MW01293663

IBM DB2 SQL for Beginners

A Practical Tutorial by Examples

Djoni Darmawikarta

Introduction

Welcome to *IBM DB2 SQL for Beginners*. This book is for you if you want to learn SQL in the IBM DB2 database the easy way. SQL, which stands for Structured Query Language and is pronounced es-cue-el, is the standard language you use to interact with a relational database management system (RDBMS). This book uses the free edition of the IBM DB2 database called Express-C Edition to show how SQL works in DB2.

SQL Overview

Initially developed at IBM in the early 1970s, SQL was formalized by the American National Standards Institute (ANSI) in 1986. Since then the SQL standard has been revised seven times. The SQL examples in this book were tested using DB2 Express-C version 10.5, which conforms to the SQL 92 standard.

SQL consists of a data definition language (DDL) and a data manipulation language (DML). The DDL is used to create, delete, and alter the structure of a table and other database objects. The DML is used to insert, retrieve, and update data in a table or tables.

Many database vendors implement a version of SQL that is not 100% compliant with the standard. They often add unique features to their SQL, resulting in an SQL dialect. For example, the following are some of the differences between DB2, Oracle and MySQL.

- The AS reserved word in the CREATE TABLE AS SELECT statement is mandatory in DB2 and Oracle, but optional in MySQL
- An INSERT statement in DB2 and MySQL can insert multiple rows; an Oracle INSERT statement can only insert one row.
- DB2 and Oracle supports UNION, INTERSECT and EXCEPT set operators; whereas MySQL only supports UNION.
- DB2 and Oracle support PL/SQL, the procedural language extension originally available only in Oracle. MySQL procedural language extension to SQL is implemented in its stored routine (MySQL did not give a name to its procedural language extension). PL/SQL has much more functions than the stored routine.

Because of these dialects, SQL statements written for one RDBMS may not necessarily work in other RDBMS's.

About This Book

This book consists of eleven chapters and three appendixes. This section gives you an overview of each chapter and appendix.

Chapter 1, "Storing and Maintaining Data" starts the book by discussing how data is stored and maintained in a relational database. In this chapter you learn how to use SQL INSERT, UPDATE, and DELETE statements.

Chapter 2, "Basic Queries" explains how to construct queries using the SELECT statement.

Chapter 3, "Query Output" shows how you can format query outputs beyond simply displaying columns of data from a database.

Chapter 4, "Grouping" explains what a group is, how to create a group, and how to apply aggregate functions to a group.

Chapter 5, "Joins" talks about the JOIN clause for querying data from multiple tables.

Chapter 6, "Subqueries" discusses the subquery. A subquery is a query that can be nested in another query.

Chapter 7, "Compound Queries" talks about set operators for combining the outputs of multiple queries.

Chapter 8, "Views" discusses views, which are predefined queries that you create and store in a database.

Chapter 9, "Built-in Functions" discusses some of the most commonly used built-in functions in the DB2 database.

Chapter 10, "PL/SQL" introduces DB2's PL/SQL programming language. PL/SQL extends SQL.

Chapter 11, "Catalog" shows how to use the data dictionary, the metadata of a database, to find information about tables, their columns, and about other objects in the database.

Appendix A, "Installing IBM DB2 Express-C" is a guide to installing DB2 Express-C Edition and making preparations for trying out the book examples.

Appendix B, "DB2 Data Types" provides a list of DB2 built-in data types.

Finally, Appendix C, "Indexing" covers the various indexing techniques available in the DB2 database.

Coding Convention of Examples

SQL is not case sensitive. In this book, however, SQL reserved words such as CREATE and SELECT and keywords such as COUNT and MAX are written in upper case. To find the complete SQL reserved words, please refer to the DB2 SQL manuals. Non-reserved words, such as table and column names, are written in lower case.

In the book examples a single space is used between words or expressions. Extra spaces are allowed and have no effect.

Chapter 1: Storing and Maintaining Data

Data in a relational database (such as the IBM DB2 database) is stored in tables. A very simple sales database, for example, might have four tables that store data on products, customers, suppliers, and customer orders.

When you add a record of data into a table, the record is stored as a row of the table. A record has fields. A product record, for example, might have four fields: product code, name, price, and launch date. All records you store in the product table must have the same fields. Each of the fields is a column of the table.

This chapter shows you how to use SQL statements to store and maintain data. The main objective of this chapter is to give you a taste of working with SQL.

To test the book examples you need a working DB2database. Appendix A, "Installing IBM DB2 Express-C" shows how you can install DB2 Express-C Edition and make it ready for use with the examples. This appendix also shows you how to start the CLPPlus command-line tool to interactively execute your SQL statements. If you do not have a working DB2 installation, you should read this appendix first.

Selecting a Database to Use

You need a database to store your data. When you install DB2 Express-C, a database named "SAMPLE" is created as part of the installation. To use this database, run CLPPlus and issue a CONNECT command as described in Appendix A, "Installing IBM DB2 Express-C."

Creating a Table

Before you can store data in a database, you must first create a table for your data. You do this by using the SQL CREATE TABLE statement. Tables that you create will reside in the database that you are currently connected to, which in this case is the SAMPLE database.

The syntax for the CREATE TABLE statement is as follows.

```
CREATE TABLE database_name.table_name
   (column_1 data_type_1,
    column_2 data_type_2,
    ...
    PRIMARY KEY (columns)
);
```

If you want to create tables in your default database (the database in your CONNECT command) you do not need to qualify the table name with the database name. From now on, the book examples will use SAMPLE as our default database.

Listing 1.1 shows a CREATE TABLE statement for creating a product table with four columns.

Listing 1.1: Creating a product table with four columns

```
CREATE TABLE product
  (
    p_code    VARCHAR (6) NOT NULL,
    p_name    VARCHAR (15),
    price     DECIMAL(4,2),
    launch_dt DATE,
    PRIMARY KEY (p_code)
  );
```

The four columns have three different data types. They are as follows.

- VARCHAR (n) – variable length string up to n characters.
- DECIMAL(p, s) – numeric with precision p and scale s. The price column, whose type is DECIMAL(4,2), can store numbers between -99.99 and +99.99.
- DATE – date

Note
Appendix B, "DB2 Data Types" has more information about DB2 data types.

When creating a table, you should always add a primary key, even though a primary key is optional. A primary key is a column or a set of columns that uniquely identify every row in the table. In the CREATE TABLE statement in Listing 1.1, the p_code field will be made the primary key for the product table.

Note that a primary key must have a value; it cannot be NULL (no value), hence the NOT NULL is specified on the p_code column.

Also note that to get it executed an SQL statement must be terminated with a semicolon (;)

Adding Data

Once you have a table, you can add data to it using the INSERT statement. The syntax for the INSERT statement is as follows

```
INSERT INTO table
   (column_1,
    column_2,
    ... )
VALUES (value_1,
        value_2,
    ... )
);
```

For example, Listing 1.2 shows an SQL statement that inserts a row into the product table.

Listing 1.2: Inserting a row into the product table

```
INSERT INTO product
  ( p_code, p_name, price, launch_dt)
  VALUES ( 1, 'Nail', 10.0, '2013-03-31');
```

After you execute the statement in Listing 1.2, your product table will have one row. You can query to find out the rows of your table using this statement.

```
SELECT * FROM product;
```

The query result will be as follows.

```
P_CODE P_NAME           PRICE LAUNCH_DT
------ ---------------- ------ ----------
1      Nail             10.00 2013-03-31
```

You can insert more than one row in an INSERT statement. The INSERT statement in Listing 1.3 adds five more rows to the product table.

Listing 1.3: Adding five more rows to the product table

```
INSERT INTO product (p_code, p_name, price, launch_dt)
  VALUES (2, 'Washer', 15.00, '2013-03-29'),
  (3, 'Nut', 15.00, '2013-03-29'),
  (4, 'Screw', 25.00, '2013-03-30'),
  (5, 'Super_Nut', 30.00, '2013-03-30'),
  (6, 'New Nut', NULL, NULL);
```

After executing the statement in Listing 1.3, your product table will contain these rows.

```
P_CODE P_NAME           PRICE LAUNCH_DT
------ ---------------- ------ ----------
1      Nail             10.00 2013-03-31
2      Washer           15.00 2013-03-29
3      Nut              15.00 2013-03-29
4      Screw            25.00 2013-03-30
```

```
5        Super_Nut         30.00 2013-03-30
6        New Nut           NULL NULL
```

Now issue a COMMIT command to persist (confirm the storage of) the additional five rows.

```
COMMIT;
```

Updating Data

You use the UPDATE statement to update one or more columns of existing data. You can update all rows in a table or certain rows in the table.

The syntax for the UPDATE statement is as follows

```
UPDATE table_name
SET column_1 = new_value_1 [,
    column_2 = new_value_2,
    ... ]
[WHERE condition];
```

You specify which rows to update in the WHERE clause. Without a WHERE clause, all rows will be updated. With a WHERE clause, only rows that meet the condition will be updated. If no row meets the condition in the WHERE clause, nothing will be updated.

As an example, the SQL statement in Listing 1.4 will cut the price by 5%. As the UPDATE statement does not have a WHERE clause, the prices of all the products will be updated.

Before you execute Listing 1.4, issue a SET AUTOCOMMIT 0; command.

Listing 1.4: Updating the price column

```
UPDATE product
SET price = price - (price * 0.05);
```

If you query the product table using this statement, you will learn that the values in the price column have changed.

```
SELECT * FROM product;
```

Here is the result of the query.

```
P_CODE P_NAME          PRICE LAUNCH_DT
------ --------------- ----- ----------
1      Nail             9.50 2013-03-31
2      Washer          14.25 2013-03-29
3      Nut             14.25 2013-03-29
```

```
4        Screw            23.75 2013-03-30
5        Super_Nut        28.50 2013-03-30
6        New Nut           NULL NULL
```

Now, issue a ROLLBACK command to return the data values back to before the update:

```
ROLLBACK;
```

As another example, the statement in Listing 1.5 will update the price of product with p_code = 9, but the product table does not have such a p_code. Therefore, no row will be updated.

Listing 1.5: Updating the price column with a WHERE clause

```
UPDATE product
SET price = price - (price * 0.05)
WHERE p_code = 9;
```

Deleting Data

To delete a row or multiple rows in a table, use the DELETE statement. You can specify which rows to be deleted by using the WHERE clause.

The syntax for the DELETE statement is as follows

```
DELETE FROM table
[WHERE condition];
```

You specify which rows to delete in the WHERE clause.

For example, the statement in Listing 1.6 deletes from the product table all rows whose p_name field value is 'Nut'.

Listing 1.6: Deleting rows

```
DELETE FROM product
WHERE p_name = 'Nut';
```

After you run the statement in Listing 1. 6, please issue a ROLLBACK command to return the data values back to before the deletion:

```
ROLLBACK;
```

If none of the rows meets the condition, nothing will be deleted. Without the WHERE condition, all rows will be deleted and the product table will be empty.

As another example, the SQL statement in Listing 1.7 deletes all the rows in the product table. If you really execute this statement, please issue a ROLLBACK statement to get back all the rows before their deletion.

Listing 1.7: Deleting all rows

```
DELETE FROM product;
```

Note that you cannot delete some of the columns in a row; the DELETE statement deletes the whole row. If you need to delete the content of a specific column, use the UPDATE statement. For instance, the statement in Listing 1.8 deletes the content of the price column. (NULL is the absence of a value; it is neither 0 (zero) or empty.) Chapter 2, "Basic Queries" has a section ("Handling NULL") that explains NULL in detail.

Listing 1.8: Updating to NULL

```
UPDATE product SET price = NULL WHERE p_name = 'Nut';
```

When you query the Nut product, the result will show NULL on the price column.

```
SELECT * FROM product WHERE p_name = 'Nut';
```

The output is as follows.

```
P_CODE P_NAME  PRICE LAUNCH_DT
------ ------ ------ ---------
1        Nut    NULL   13-DEC-01
```

Please issue a ROLLBACK command to return the data values back to before the update:

```
ROLLBACK;
```

Summary

In this chapter you got the first taste of working with SQL. You learned how to create a table and store data. In Chapter 2, "Basic Queries" you will learn to use the SELECT statement to query data.

Chapter 2: Basic Queries

A query is a request for data from one or more tables. When you execute a query, rows that satisfy the condition of the query will be returned as a table. Similarly, when a query embedded in another query or a program gets executed, the data returned to the other query or the program is a table.

In this chapter you learn how to write basic queries using the SELECT statement. Once you master the basic queries, you can start learning about queries within other queries in Chapter 6, "Subqueries" and within PL/SQL programs in Chapter 10, "PL/SQL"

The SELECT statement

All queries regardless of their complexity use the SELECT statement. The SELECT statement has the following general syntax.

```
SELECT column_names FROM table_name [WHERE condition];
```

Only the SELECT and FROM clauses are mandatory. If your query does not have a WHERE clause, the result will include all rows in the table. If your query has a WHERE clause then only the rows satisfying the WHERE condition will be returned.

Querying All Data

The simplest query, which reads all data (all rows and all columns) from a table, has the following syntax.

```
SELECT * FROM table;
```

The asterisk (*) means all columns in the table. For instance, Listing 2.1 shows an SQL statement that queries all data from the product table.

Listing 2.1: Querying all product data

```
SELECT * FROM product;
```

Executing the query will give you the following result.

```
P_CODE P_NAME            PRICE LAUNCH_DT
```

```
------  ---------------  ------  ----------
1       Nail             10.00   2013-03-31
2       Washer           15.00   2013-03-29
3       Nut              15.00   2013-03-29
4       Screw            25.00   2013-03-30
5       Super_Nut        30.00   2013-03-30
6       New Nut          NULL    NULL
```

Selecting Specific Columns

To query specific columns, list the columns in the SELECT clause. You write the columns in the order you want to see them in the output table. For example, the SELECT statement in Listing 2.2 queries the p_name and the price columns from the product table.

Listing 2.2: Querying specific columns

```
SELECT p_name, price FROM product;
```

All rows containing p_name and price columns will be returned by the query. Here is the query output.

```
P_NAME                  PRICE
---------------         ------
Nail                    10.00
Washer                  15.00
Nut                     15.00
Screw                   25.00
Super_Nut               30.00
New Nut                 NULL
```

Selecting Rows with WHERE

To query specific rows, use the WHERE clause. Recall that the SQL SELECT statement has the following syntax.

```
SELECT column_names FROM table_name [WHERE condition];
```

For example, the SQL statement in Listing 2.3 queries the p_name and price data from the product table with price = 15.

Listing 2.3: Querying specific rows

```
SELECT p_name, price FROM product WHERE price = 15;
```

Only rows whose price is 15 will be returned by the query, in this case the Washer and Nut. The query output is as follows.

```
P_NAME                  PRICE
---------------         ------
```

```
Washer          15.00
Nut             15.00
```

The equal sign (=) in the WHERE condition in Listing 2.3 is one of the comparison operators. Table 2.1 shows all comparison operators.

Operator	Description
=	Equal to
<	Less than
>	Greater than
<=	Less than or equal to
>=	Greater than or equal to
!=	Not equal to

Table 2.1: Comparison operators

As another example, Listing 2.4 shows a WHERE clause that uses the not equal to (!=) operator.

Listing 2.4: Using the != comparison operator

```
SELECT p_name, price FROM product WHERE p_name != 'Nut';
```

Only rows whose p_name is not Nut will be returned by the query. In this case, the query output will be as follows.

```
P_NAME          PRICE
--------------- ------
Nail            10.00
Washer          15.00
Screw           25.00
Super_Nut       30.00
New Nut          NULL
```

Compound Conditions

The condition p_name != 'Nut' in Listing 2.4 is called a predicate. Using the AND and OR logical operator you can combine predicates to form a compound condition. Only rows that satisfy the compound condition will be returned by the query.

The rules for the OR logical operator are given in Table 2.2.

Left condition	Logical operator	Right condition	Compound condition
True	OR	True	True
True	OR	False	True
False	OR	True	True
False	OR	False	False

Table 2.2: The OR rules

In principle, the result of the OR compound condition is true (satisfying the condition) if any one of the two conditions being OR-ed is true; otherwise, if none of the conditions is true, the compound condition is false (not satisfying the condition).

The rules for the AND logical operator are presented in Table 2.3.

Left condition	Logical operator	Right condition	Compound condition
True	AND	True	True
True	AND	False	FALSE
False	AND	True	FALSE
False	AND	False	FALSE

Table 2.3: The AND rules

Basically, the result of the AND compound condition is true only if the two conditions being AND-ed are true; otherwise, the result is false.

For example, the statement in Listing 2.5 contains three predicates in its WHERE clause.

Listing 2.5: A query with three predicates

```
SELECT *
FROM product
WHERE (launch_dt >= '2013-03-30'
OR price        > 15)
AND (p_name     != 'Nail');
```

The result of the first compound condition (launch_dt >= '30-MAR-13' OR price > 15) is true for Nail, Screw and Super_Nut rows in the product table; AND-ing this result with the (p_name != 'Nail') predicate results in two products, the Screw and Super_Nut.

Here is the output of the query in Listing 2.5:

```
P_CODE P_NAME          PRICE LAUNCH_DT
------ --------------- ------ ----------
4      Screw           25.00 2013-03-30
5      Super_Nut       30.00 2013-03-30
```

Note that New Nut does not satisfy the condition because applying any of the comparison operators to NULL results in false (the price and launch_dt of the New Nut are NULL). The section "Handling NULL" later in this chapter explains more about NULL.

Evaluation Precedence and the Use of Parentheses

If a compound condition contains both the OR condition and the AND condition, the AND condition will be evaluated first because AND has a higher precedence than OR. However, anything in parentheses will have an even higher precedence than AND. For example, the SELECT statement in Listing 2.5 has an OR and an AND, but the OR condition is in parentheses so the OR condition is evaluated first. If you remove the parentheses in the SELECT statement in Listing 2.5, the query will return a different result. Consider the statement in Listing 2.6, which is similar to that in Listing 2.5 except that the parentheses have been removed.

Listing 2.6: Evaluation precedence

```
SELECT *
FROM product
WHERE launch_dt >= '2013-03-30'
OR price        > 15
AND p_name      != 'Nail';
```

For your reading convenience, the product table is reprinted here.

P_CODE	P_NAME	PRICE	LAUNCH_DT
1	Nail	10.00	31-MAR-13
2	Washer	15.00	29-MAR-13
3	Nut	15.00	29-MAR-13
4	Screw	25.00	30-MAR-13
5	Super_Nut	30.00	30-MAR-13
6	New Nut	NULL	NULL

Without the parentheses, the compound condition price > 15 AND p_name != 'Nail' will be evaluated first, resulting in the Screw and Super_Nut. The result is then OR-ed with the launch_dt >= 30-MAR-13' condition, resulting in these three rows.

P_CODE	P_NAME	PRICE	LAUNCH_DT
1	Nail	10.00	2013-03-31
4	Screw	25.00	2013-03-30
5	Super_Nut	30.00	2013-03-30

The NOT logical operator

You can use NOT to negate a condition and return rows that do not satisfy the condition. Consider the query in Listing 2.7.

Listing 2.7: Using the NOT operator

```
SELECT *
FROM product
WHERE NOT (launch_dt >= '2013-03-30'
OR price          > 15
AND p_name        != 'Nail' );
```

Thanks to the NOT operator in the query in Listing 2.7, the two rows not satisfying the condition in Listing 2.6 will now be returned.

```
P_CODE P_NAME            PRICE LAUNCH_DT
------ ---------------- ------ ----------
2      Washer           15.00 2013-03-29
3      Nut              15.00 2013-03-29
```

As another example, the query in Listing 2.8 negates the last predicate only (as opposed to the previous query that negated the overall WHERE condition).

Listing 2.8: Using NOT on one predicate

```
SELECT *
FROM product
WHERE (launch_dt >= '2013-03-30'
OR price        > 15)
AND NOT (p_name  != 'Nail');
```

The output of the query in Listing 2.8 is as follows.

```
P_CODE P_NAME            PRICE LAUNCH_DT
------ ---------------- ------ ----------
1      Nail             10.00 2013-03-31
```

The BETWEEN Operator

The BETWEEN operator evaluates equality to any value within a range. The range is specified by a boundary, which specifies the lowest and the highest values.

Here is the syntax for BETWEEN.

```
SELECT columns FROM table
WHERE column BETWEEN(lowest_value, highest_value);
```

The boundary values are inclusive, meaning *lowest_value* and *highest_value* will be included in the equality evaluation.

For example, the query in Listing 2.9 uses the BETWEEN operator to specify the lowest and highest prices that need to be returned from the product table.

Listing 2.9: Using the BETWEEN operator

```
SELECT * FROM product WHERE price BETWEEN 15 AND 25;
```

Here is the output of the query in Listing 2.9.

```
P_CODE P_NAME           PRICE LAUNCH_DT
------ ---------------- ------ ----------
2      Washer           15.00 2013-03-29
3      Nut              15.00 2013-03-29
4      Screw            25.00 2013-03-30
```

The IN Operator

The IN operator compares a column with a list of values. The syntax for a query that uses IN is as follows.

```
SELECT columns FROM table
WHERE column IN(value1, value2, ...);
```

For example, the query in Listing 2.10 uses the IN operator to select all columns whose price is in the list (10, 25, 50).

Listing 2.10: Using the IN operator

```
SELECT * FROM product WHERE price IN (10, 25, 50);
```

The output of the query in Listing 2.10 is as follows.

```
P_CODE P_NAME           PRICE LAUNCH_DT
------ ---------------- ------ ----------
1      Nail             10.00 2013-03-31
4      Screw            25.00 2013-03-30
```

The LIKE Operator

The LIKE operator allows you to specify an imprecise equality condition. The syntax is as follows.

```
SELECT columns FROM table
WHERE column LIKE ' ... wildcard_character ... ';
```

The wildcard character can be a percentage sign (%) to represent any number of characters or an underscore (_) to represent a single occurrence of any character.

As an example, the query in Listing 2.11 uses the LIKE operator to find products whose name starts with Sc and can be of any length.

Listing 2.11: Using the LIKE operator with %

```
SELECT * FROM product WHERE p_name LIKE 'Sc%';
```

The output of the query in Listing 2.11 is this.

```
P_CODE P_NAME            PRICE LAUNCH_DT
------ ---------------   ------ ----------
4      Screw              25.00 2013-03-30
```

The query in Listing 2.12 uses the LIKE operator to find products whose name starts with N and is followed by two characters.

Listing 2.12: Using the LIKE operator with __

```
SELECT * FROM product WHERE p_name LIKE 'N__';
```

The output of the query in Listing 2.12 is this.

```
P_CODE P_NAME            PRICE LAUNCH_DT

------ ---------------   ------ ----------

3      Nut                15.00 2013-03-29
```

Even though you can use LIKE for numeric columns, it is primarily used with columns of type string.

Escaping the Wildcard Character

If the string you specify in the LIKE operator contains an underscore or a percentage sign, SQL will regard it as a wild character. For example, if you want to query products that have an underscore in their names, your SQL statement would look like that in Listing 2.12.

Listing 2.13: A wildcard character _ in the LIKE string

```
SELECT * FROM product WHERE p_name LIKE '%_%';
```

If you execute the query in Listing 2.13, the query will return all rows instead of just the Super_Nut, because the underscore in the LIKE operator is regarded as a wild card character, i.e. any one character. Listing 2.13 resolves this problem by prefixing the wild card character with the \ (backslash) escape character, meaning any character in the LIKE operator after a backslash will be considered a character, not as a wildcard character. Now only rows whose p_name contains an underscore will be returned.

Listing 2.14: Escaping the wildcard character _

```
SELECT * FROM product WHERE p_name LIKE '%\_%' ESCAPE
      '\';
```

The query in Listing 2.14 will produce the following output.

```
P_CODE  P_NAME           PRICE LAUNCH_DT
------  ---------------  ------ ----------
5       Super_Nut        30.00 2013-03-30
```

Combining the NOT operator

You can combine NOT with BETWEEN, IN, or LIKE to negate their conditions. For example, the query in Listing 2.14 uses NOT with BETWEEN.

Listing 2.15: Using NOT with BETWEEN

```
SELECT * FROM product WHERE price NOT BETWEEN 15 AND 25;
```

Executing the query in Listing 2.15 will give you this result.

```
P_CODE  P_NAME           PRICE LAUNCH_DT
------  ---------------  ------ ----------
1       Nail             10.00 2013-03-31
5       Super_Nut        30.00 2013-03-30
```

Handling NULL

NULL, an SQL reserved word, represents the absence of data. NULL is applicable to any data type. It is not the same as a numeric zero or an empty string or a 0000/00/00 date. You can specify whether or not a column can be null in the CREATE TABLE statement for creating the table.

The result of applying any of the comparison operators on NULL is always NULL. You can only test whether or not a column is NULL by using the IS NULL or IS NOT NULL operator.

Consider the query in Listing 2.16.

Listing 2.16: Invalid usage of the equal operator on NULL

```
SELECT * FROM product WHERE price = NULL;
```

Executing the query in Listing 2.16 produces no output. In fact, you will get the following message.

No rows were retrieved. As another example, consider the query in Listing 2.17 that uses IS NULL.

Listing 2.17: Using IS NULL

```
SELECT * FROM product WHERE price IS NULL;
```

The query output is as follows.

```
P_CODE  P_NAME           PRICE  LAUNCH_DT
------  ---------------  ------  ----------
6       New Nut           NULL  NULL
```

Note

Chapter 6, "Built-in Functions," discusses functions that you can use to test column nullity.

Summary

In this chapter you learned the basics queries using the SELECT statement. In the next chapter you will learn how to format query outputs.

Chapter 3: Query Output

All the queries in Chapter 2, "Basic Queries" returned rows that contained columns from the source table. However, output rows can also contain string or numeric expressions that include string or numeric literals, operators, and functions.

In this chapter you learn how to manipulate query output using expressions and how to order and store output rows into a table.

Column Aliases

By default the names of the output columns in the query output are the names of the columns of the queried table. However, you don't have to be stuck with the original column names. You can give them different names or aliases if you wish.

The syntax for the SELECT clause that uses aliases is as follows.

```
SELECT column_1 AS alias1, column_2 AS alias2, ...
FROM table;
```

An alias can consist of one or multiple words. You must enclose a multiword alias with quotes, e.g. "PRODUCT NAME". For example, the query in Listing 3.1 uses an alias for the p_name column.

Listing 3.1: Using an alias in a query

```
SELECT p_code,
  p_name AS "PRODUCT NAME"
FROM product;
```

Expressions

An output column can also be an expression. An expression in the SELECT clause can include columns, literal values, arithmetic or string operators, and functions. For instance, the SELECT clause in the query in Listing 3.2 employs several expressions.

Listing 3.2: Various types of output columns

```
SELECT p_code,
  UPPER(p_name))                    AS "PRODUCT NAME",
  (price * 100)                     AS "PRICE*100",
```

```
    VARCHAR_FORMAT(launch_dt, 'DD/MM/YYYY') AS
        "LAUNCH_DATE"
FROM product;
```

The output of the query in Listing 3.2 will have four columns.

The first output column, p_code, is a column from the product table.

The second output column (aliased "PRODUCT NAME") is an expression UPPER(p_name), where UPPER is a function applied to the p_name column from the product table. The UPPER function changes the case of the product names to uppercase.

The third output column ("PRICE*100") is an arithmetic expression (price*100).

The last output column ("LAUNCH_DATE") is the launch_date column formatted as DD/MM/YYYY.

Applied against the following product table

```
P_CODE  P_NAME           PRICE  LAUNCH_DT
------  ---------------  -----  ---- ----
1       Nail             10.00  31-MAR-13
2       Washer           15.00  29-MAR-13
3       Nut              15.00  29-MAR-13
4       Screw            25.00  30-MAR-13
5       Super_Nut        30.00  30-MAR-13
6       New Nut           NULL  NULL
```

the query in Listing 3.2 returns the following rows.

```
P_CODE  PRODUCT NAME             PRICE*100  LAUNCH_DATE
------  ---------------  ------------------  ---------------
1       NAIL                       1000.00  31/03/13
2       WASHER                     1500.00  29/03/13
3       NUT                        1500.00  29/03/13
4       SCREW                      2500.00  30/03/13
5       SUPER_NUT                  3000.00  30/03/13
6       NEW NUT                       NULL  NULL
```

You can use other arithmetic operators in addition to the multiplication (*) operator in your column. These include addition (+), subtraction (-), and division (/)

Note
Chapter 9, "Built-in Functions" explains functions in more detail.

Limiting the Number of Rows

You can limit the number of output row by using the FETCH FIRST ROWS ONLY clause. Its syntax is as follows.

```
SELECT columns FROM table(s)
WHERE conditions FETCH FIRST n ROWS ONLY;
```

The maximum number of output rows of a query that employs the FETCH FIRST ROWS ONLY will be *n*.

As an example, take a look at the query in Listing 3.3.

Listing 3.3: Using FETCH FIRST

SELECT * FROM product WHERE price > 10 FETCH FIRST 3 ROWS ONLY;

Without the expression FETCH FIRST 3 ROWS ONLY, the number of output rows would be 4. The query in Listing 3.3, however, returns these three rows.

```
P_CODE  P_NAME           PRICE LAUNCH_DT
------  ---------------- ------ ----------
2       Washer           15.00 2013-03-29
3       Nut              15.00 2013-03-29
4       Screw            25.00 2013-03-30
```

The DISTINCT Keyword

A query may return duplicate rows. Two rows are duplicates if each of their columns contains exactly the same data. If you don't want to see duplicate output rows, use DISTINCT in your SELECT clause. You can use DISTINCT on one column or multiple columns.

Using DISTINCT on A Single Column

The query in Listing 3.4 uses DISTINCT on the price column.

Listing 3.4: Using DISTINCT on a single column

SELECT DISTINCT price FROM product ORDER BY price;

Without DISTINCT, the query in Listing 3.4 will return six rows that include two duplicate prices for row 2 and row 3. Instead, the query in Listing 3.4 returns the following output.

```
PRICE
```

```
------
 10.00
 15.00
 25.00
 30.00
  NULL
```

Using DISTINCT on Multiple Columns

If a query returns multiple columns, two rows are considered duplicates if all their columns have the same values. They are not duplicates if only one column has the same value.

The DISTINCT keyword can be applied on multiple columns too. For example, the query in Listing 3.5 uses DISTINCT on multiple columns.

Listing 3.5: Using DISTINCT on multiple columns

```
SELECT DISTINCT price, launch_dt FROM product ORDER BY
     price;
```

Here is the output. Note that output rows with the same price and launch_dt will only be shown once.

```
PRICE LAUNCH_DT
------ ----------
 10.00 2013-03-31
 15.00 2013-03-29
 25.00 2013-03-30
 30.00 2013-03-30
  NULL NULL
```

Aggregate Functions

You can manipulate your query output further by using aggregate functions. The aggregate functions are listed in Table 3.1.

Function	Description
MAX(column)	The maximum column value
MIN(column)	The minimum column value
SUM(column)	The sum of column values
AVG(column)	The average column value
COUNT(column)	The count of rows
COUNT(*)	The count of all rows including NULL.

Table 3.1: Built-in aggregate functions

As an example, the query in Listing 3.6 uses the aggregate functions in Table 3.1.

Listing 3.6: Using aggregate functions

```
SELECT MAX(price) max,
  MIN(price) min,
  SUM(price) sum,
  AVG(price) avg,
  COUNT(price) "count(price)",
  COUNT(*)"count(*)"
FROM product;
```

Note that only COUNT(*) takes into account the New Nut product because its price is NULL.

The output of the query in Listing 3.6 is this.

```
   MAX    MIN    SUM    AVG COUNT(PRICE)     COUNT(*)
 ------ ------ ------ ------ ------------- -----------
  30.00  10.00  95.00  19.00             5            6
```

The CASE expression

CASE allows you to have dynamic query output in which a column value may vary depending on the value of the column. CASE comes in two flavors: Simple and Searched. Both will be explained in the following subsections.

The Simple CASE

The general syntax for the Simple CASE is as follows.

```
SELECT columns,
  CASE column
    WHEN equal_value1
    THEN output_value1
    WHEN equal_value2
    THEN output_value2
    WHEN ...
    [ELSE else_value]
  END AS output_column
FROM table
WHERE ... ;
```

In the Simple CASE, *column_name* is compared to *equal_value*s in the WHEN clause, starting from the first WHEN and down to the last WHEN. If *column_name* matches a WHEN value, the value right after the THEN clause is returned and the CASE process stops. If *column_name* matches none of the WHEN values, *else_value* is returned if there exists an ELSE clause. If *column_name* matches none of the WHEN values but no ELSE clause exists, NULL will be returned.

As an example, the query in Listing 3.7 uses a Simple CASE expression for the price column to produce a price_cat (price category) output column.

Listing 3.7: An example of the Simple CASE

```
SELECT p_code,
  p_name,
  CASE price
    WHEN 10
    THEN 'Cheap'
    WHEN 15
    THEN 'Medium'
    WHEN 25
    THEN 'Expensive'
    ELSE 'Others'
  END AS price_cat
FROM product;
```

Assuming the product table has the following data

```
P_CODE P_NAME           PRICE LAUNCH_DT
------ --------------- ------ ----------
1      Nail             10.00 2013-03-31
2      Washer           15.00 2013-03-29
3      Nut              15.00 2013-03-29
4      Screw            25.00 2013-03-30
5      Super_Nut        30.00 2013-03-30
6      New Nut           NULL NULL
```

the query will return these rows.

```
P_CODE P_NAME          PRICE_CAT
------ --------------- ---------
1      Nail            Cheap
2      Washer          Medium
3      Nut             Medium
4      Screw           Expensive
5      Super_Nut       Others
6      New Nut         Others
```

The Searched CASE

The case in the Simple CASE compares a column with various values. On the hand, the case in the Searched CASE can be any condition. Here is the syntax for the Searched CASE.

```
SELECT columns,
  CASE
    WHEN condition1
    THEN output_value1
    WHEN condition2
    THEN output_value2
    WHEN ...
    ELSE else_value
  END AS output_column
FROM table
WHERE ... ;
```

The conditions are evaluated starting from the first WHEN and down to the last WHEN. If a WHEN condition is met, its THEN output_value is returned to the output_column and the CASE process stops. If none of the WHEN conditions is met, *else_value* is returned if there exists an ELSE clause. If no condition is met and no ELSE clause exists, NULL will be returned.

For instance, the query in Listing 3.8 uses a Searched CASE. While the Simple CASE in Listing 3.7 categorized the products based on only their prices, this Searched CASE categorizes the products based on the various conditions which can involve more than just the price. Note that in the Search CASE, NULL equality can be a condition, something that is not allowed in the Simple CASE.

Listing 3.8: An example of the Searched CASE

```
SELECT p_code,
  p_name,
  CASE
    WHEN (price <= 10
    AND p_name NOT LIKE 'Nut%')
    THEN 'Cheap'
    WHEN price BETWEEN 11 AND 25
    THEN 'Medium'
    WHEN price > 25 and TO_CHAR(launch_dt, 'YYYYMMDD') >
      '20130329'
    THEN 'Expensive'
    WHEN price IS NULL
    THEN 'Not valid'
    ELSE 'Others'
  END AS product_cat
FROM product;
```

Applying the query against the following product table

```
P_CODE P_NAME           PRICE LAUNCH_DT
------ ---------------- ------ ----------
1      Nail             10.00 2013-03-31
```

```
2        Washer              15.00 2013-03-29
3        Nut                 15.00 2013-03-29
4        Screw               25.00 2013-03-30
5        Super_Nut           30.00 2013-03-30
6        New Nut              NULL NULL
```

will return the following rows.

```
P_CODE  P_NAME              PRODUCT_CAT
------  ---------------     -----------
1       Nail                Cheap
2       Washer              Medium
3       Nut                 Medium
4       Screw               Medium
5       Super_Nut           Expensive
6       New Nut             Not valid
```

Ordering Output Rows

To provide better visualization of the output, you can order output rows based on certain criteria. To order the output, use the ORDER BY clause. The ORDER BY clause must appear last in a SELECT statement.

Here is the syntax for a query having the ORDER BY clause.

```
SELECT columns FROM
table
WHERE condition ORDER BY column(s)
```

You can order output rows in one of the following methods.

- by one or more columns
- in ascending or descending direction
- by using the GROUP BY clause
- by using UNION and other set operators

Each of the methods is explained in the subsections below.

Ordering by One Column

To order your query output rows, use the ORDER BY clause with one column. For instance, have a look at the query in Listing 3.9.

Listing 3.9: Ordering by one column

```
SELECT * FROM product ORDER BY p_name;
```

When you apply the query against the following product table

```
P_CODE  P_NAME              PRICE LAUNCH_DT
```

```
------ --------------- ------ ----------
1      Nail            10.00 2013-03-31
2      Washer          15.00 2013-03-29
3      Nut             15.00 2013-03-29
4      Screw           25.00 2013-03-30
5      Super_Nut       30.00 2013-03-30
6      New Nut          NULL NULL
```

you will see the following output.

```
P_CODE P_NAME          PRICE LAUNCH_DT
------ --------------- ------ ----------
1      Nail            10.00 2013-03-31
6      New Nut          NULL NULL
3      Nut             15.00 2013-03-29
4      Screw           25.00 2013-03-30
5      Super_Nut       30.00 2013-03-30
2      Washer          15.00 2013-03-29
```

Direction of Order

The default direction is ascending. To order a column in descending direction, use the DESC reserved word. For example, the query in Listing 3.10 is similar to that in Listing 3.9 except that the output is presented in descending order.

Listing 3.10: Changing the order direction

```
SELECT * FROM product ORDER BY p_name DESC;
```

The output rows will be returned with p_name sorted in descending order.

```
P_CODE P_NAME          PRICE LAUNCH_DT
------ --------------- ------ ----------
2      Washer          15.00 2013-03-29
5      Super_Nut       30.00 2013-03-30
4      Screw           25.00 2013-03-30
3      Nut             15.00 2013-03-29
6      New Nut          NULL NULL
1      Nail            10.00 2013-03-31
```

Multiple Columns

To order by more than one column, list the columns in the ORDER BY clause. The sequence of columns listed is significant. The order will be conducted by the first column in the list, followed by the second column, and so on. For example, if the ORDER BY clause has two columns, the query output will first be ordered by the first column. Any rows with identical values in the first column will be further ordered by the second column.

For example, the query in Listing 3.11 uses an ORDER BY clause with two columns.

Listing 3.11: Multiple column ordering

```
SELECT * FROM product ORDER BY launch_dt, price;
```

Applying the query against the product table.

```
P_CODE P_NAME            PRICE LAUNCH_DT
------ ---------------   ------ ----------
1      Nail              10.00 2013-03-31
2      Washer            15.00 2013-03-29
3      Nut               15.00 2013-03-29
4      Screw             25.00 2013-03-30
5      Super_Nut         30.00 2013-03-30
6      New Nut            NULL NULL
```

The output rows will first be ordered by launch_dt and then by price, both in ascending order. The secondary ordering by price is seen on the Screw and Super_Nut rows. Their launch_dt's are the same, 30-MAR-13. Their prices are different, Screw's lower than Super_Nut's, hence Screw row comes before the Super_Nut.

```
P_CODE P_NAME            PRICE LAUNCH_DT
------ ---------------   ------ ----------
2      Washer            15.00 2013-03-29
3      Nut               15.00 2013-03-29
4      Screw             25.00 2013-03-30
5      Super_Nut         30.00 2013-03-30
1      Nail              10.00 2013-03-31
6      New Nut            NULL NULL
```

Different Directions on Different Columns

You can apply different order directions on ordered columns too. For example, the query in Listing 3.12 uses different directions on different columns in its ORDER BY clause.

Listing 3.12: Using multiple directions of ORDER

```
SELECT * FROM product ORDER BY launch_dt, price DESC;
```

Applying the query against the product table, the output rows will be ordered by launch_dt in ascending order and then by price in descending order. Now, the Super_Nut comes before the Screw.

```
P_CODE P_NAME            PRICE LAUNCH_DT
```

```
------  ---------------  ------  ----------
2       Washer           15.00 2013-03-29
3       Nut              15.00 2013-03-29
5       Super_Nut        30.00 2013-03-30
4       Screw            25.00 2013-03-30
1       Nail             10.00 2013-03-31
6       New Nut          NULL NULL
```

Ordering with a WHERE clause

If your SELECT statement has both the WHERE clause and the ORDER BY clause, ORDER BY must appear after the WHERE clause.

For example, the query in Listing 3.13 has both WHERE and ORDER BY. This query will return only Nut products.

Listing 3.13: Using both WHERE and ORDER BY

```
SELECT * FROM product WHERE p_name = 'Nut'
ORDER BY p_name, p_code DESC;
```

If you execute the query, you will see one row only, the Nut, in the output window.

```
P_CODE P_NAME                  PRICE LAUNCH_DT
------ ---------------  ------ ----------
3       Nut              15.00 2013-03-29
```

Storing Query Output

You can store a query output into an existing table.

To store a query output into an existing table, use this syntax.

```
INSERT INTO existing_table AS SELECT ... ;
```

For example, the query in Listing 3.14 stores the query result in an existing table.

Listing 3.14: Storing output into an existing table

```
INSERT INTO non_nut
SELECT * FROM product WHERE p_name NOT LIKE '%Nut%';
```

Before executing INSERT statement of Listing 3.15, first you have to create a non_nut table by executing the following statement.

```
CREATE TABLE non_nut
  (
    p_code     VARCHAR(6) NOT NULL,
    p_name     VARCHAR(15),
```

```
price      DECIMAL(4,2),
launch_dt DATE,
PRIMARY KEY (p_code)
);
```

Applying the query in Listing 3.15 against this product table

```
P_CODE P_NAME           PRICE LAUNCH_DT
------ ---------------- ------ ----------
1      Nail             10.00 2013-03-31
2      Washer           15.00 2013-03-29
3      Nut              15.00 2013-03-29
4      Screw            25.00 2013-03-30
5      Super_Nut        30.00 2013-03-30
6      New Nut          NULL NULL
```

the non_nut table will get the following rows.

```
P_CODE P_NAME           PRICE LAUNCH_DT
------ ---------------- ------ ----------
1      Nail             10.00 2013-03-31
2      Washer           15.00 2013-03-29
4      Screw            25.00 2013-03-30
```

Summary

SQL allows you to retrieve rows from a table and manipulate the output. You learned in this chapter that you can create aliases, use aggregate functions, and order rows.

Chapter 4: Grouping

A group is a set of rows having the same value on specific columns. In Chapter 3, "Query Output" you learned how to apply aggregate functions on all output rows. In this chapter you learn how to create groups and apply aggregate functions on those groups.

The GROUP BY Clause

In a query the GROUP BY clause appears after the WHERE clause and before the ORDER clause, if any. Here is the syntax for a SELECT statement with the WHERE, GROUP BY, and ORDER BY clauses.

```
SELECT columns,
  aggregate_function(group_columns)
FROM table(s)
```

```
WHERE condition
GROUP BY group_columns
ORDER BY column(s);
```

As an example, the query in Listing 4.1 groups the output from the product table by their launch date.

Listing 4.1: Grouping on one column

```
SELECT launch_dt,
  MAX(price) MAX ,
  MIN(price) MIN ,
  dec(SUM(price),4,2) SUM ,
  dec(AVG(price),4,2) AVG ,
  COUNT(price) CNT ,
  COUNT(*) AS "COUNT(*)"
FROM product1
GROUP BY launch_dt
ORDER BY launch_dt;
```

Applied against a product table with the following rows, aggregations will be done by the four grouped launch dates: 29, 30 and 31 of March 2013, and NULL.

```
P_CODE P_NAME            PRICE LAUNCH_DT
------ ---------------- ------ ----------
1      Nail             10.00 2013-03-31
2      Washer           15.00 2013-03-29
3      Nut              15.00 2013-03-29
4      Screw            25.00 2013-03-30
5      Super_Nut        30.00 2013-03-30
6      New Nut           NULL NULL
```

The query output will have four rows, one for each of the four grouped launch dates. Note that the COUNT(price) element, which counts the rows with a value on their price column, produces 0. On the other hand, the COUNT(*) element, which counts the NULL launch dates, produces 1.

```
LAUNCH_DT    MAX    MIN    SUM    AVG        CNT    COUNT(*)
---------- ------ ------ ------ ------ ----------- -----------
2013-03-29 15.00  15.00  30.00  15.00            2           2
2013-03-30 30.00  25.00  55.00  27.50            2           2
2013-03-31 10.00  10.00  10.00  10.00            1           1
NULL        NULL   NULL   NULL   NULL            0           1
```

You can group by more than one column. If you do that, rows having the same value on all the columns will form a group. As an example, the query in Listing 4.2 groups rows by price and launch date.

Listing 4.2: Grouping on two columns

```
SELECT launch_dt,
   MAX(price) MAX ,
   MIN(price) MIN ,
   dec(SUM(price),4,2) SUM ,
   dec(AVG(price),4,2) AVG ,
   COUNT(price) CNT ,
   COUNT(*) AS "COUNT(*)"
FROM product1
GROUP BY price, launch_dt
ORDER BY price, launch_dt;
```

Applied to the same product table, the output will have five rows. Even though the Screw and Super_Nut have the same price, they have different launch dates, and therefore form different groups.

LAUNCH_DT	MAX	MIN	SUM	AVG	CNT	COUNT(*)
2013-03-31	10.00	10.00	10.00	10.00	1	1
2013-03-29	15.00	15.00	30.00	15.00	2	2
2013-03-30	25.00	25.00	25.00	25.00	1	1
2013-03-30	30.00	30.00	30.00	30.00	1	1
NULL	NULL	NULL	NULL	NULL	0	1

The HAVING Keyword

The WHERE condition can be used to select individual rows. On the other hand, the HAVING condition is used for selecting individual groups. Only groups that satisfy the condition in the HAVING clause will be returned by the query. In other words, the HAVING condition is on the aggregate, not on a column.

If present, the HAVING clause must appear after the GROUP BY, as in the following syntax.

```
SELECT columns,
   aggregate_function(group_columns)
FROM table(s)
WHERE condition
GROUP BY group_columns
HAVING aggregate_condition
ORDER BY columns;
```

As an example, the query in Listing 4.3 uses the HAVING condition.

Listing 4.3: Using the HAVING condition

```
SELECT launch_dt,
   MAX(price) MAX ,
   MIN(price) MIN ,
```

```
  SUM(price) SUM ,
  AVG(price) AVG ,
  COUNT(price) CNT ,
  COUNT(*) AS "COUNT(*)"
FROM product
GROUP BY price, launch_dt
HAVING COUNT(price) > 1
ORDER BY price, launch_dt;
```

Only groups having more than one row (satisfying the COUNT(price) > 1 condition) will be returned. Only one row will be returned, the one with price = 15 and launch date = 29-MAR-13.

```
LAUNCH_DT    MAX    MIN    SUM    AVG         CNT   COUNT(*)
---------- ------ ------ ------ ------ ----------- -----------
2013-03-29  15.00  15.00  30.00  15.00           2           2
```

If a WHERE clause is present, it must appear after the GROUP BY clause. Individual rows will be selected by the WHERE condition first before grouping occurs. For instance, the query in Listing 4.4 uses both WHERE and GROUP BY.

Listing 4.4: Grouping with WHERE

```
SELECT launch_dt,
  MAX(price) MAX ,
  MIN(price) MIN ,
  SUM(price) SUM ,
  AVG(price) AVG ,
  COUNT(price) CNT ,
  COUNT(*) AS "COUNT(*)"
FROM product
WHERE p_name NOT LIKE 'Super%'
GROUP BY launch_dt
HAVING launch_dt > '2013-03-29'
ORDER BY launch_dt;
SELECT launch_dt,
  MAX(price) MAX ,
  MIN(price) MIN ,
  SUM(price) SUM ,
  AVG(price) AVG ,
  COUNT(price) CNT ,
  COUNT(*) AS 'C(*)'
FROM product
WHERE p_name NOT LIKE 'Super%'
GROUP BY launch_dt
HAVING launch_dt > '2013-03-29'
ORDER BY launch_dt;
```

Here is the query output.

```
LAUNCH_DT      MAX    MIN    SUM    AVG         CNT   COUNT(*)
```

```
---------- ------ ------ ------ ------ ----------- -----------
2013-03-30  25.00  25.00  25.00  25.00            1            1
2013-03-31  10.00  10.00  10.00  10.00            1            1
```

In this case, Super_Nut does not satisfy the WHERE condition. As such, it is not included in the aggregation.

Applying aggregate as a WHERE condition clause is not allowed. This is shown in Listing 4.5, which contains a query that throws an error if executed.

Listing 4.5: Error with WHERE on the aggregate

```
SELECT launch_dt,
  MAX(price) MAX ,
  MIN(price) MIN ,
  SUM(price) SUM ,
  AVG(price) AVG ,
  COUNT(price) CNT ,
  COUNT(*) AS "COUNT(*)"
FROM product
WHERE COUNT(price) > 1;
```

Executing this query will give you this error message.

```
SQL0120N Invalid use of an aggregate function or OLAP
         function.
```

Summary

In this chapter you learned how to aggregate values from rows. You also learned to use the HAVING condition applied on aggregates. In the next chapter you will learn about the JOIN clause used to "aggregate" rows from more than one table.

Chapter 5: Joins

A real-world database typically stores data in dozens or even hundreds of tables. In these multi-table databases, a table often relates to one or some other tables. In this environment, you should be able to relate rows from two or more tables by using the JOIN clause. This chapter shows you how.

Primary Keys and Foreign Keys

In Chapter 1, "Storing and Maintaining Data" you learned about primary keys. A primary key is a column, or a set of columns, which uniquely identifies every row in a table. A foreign key is a column, or a set of columns, which is used to relate to the primary key of another table. The process of using the foreign key/primary key to relate rows from two tables is called joining.

While a primary key must be unique, a foreign key does not have to be unique. You can have a foreign key in more than one row. For example, in a customer order table you can have many orders for the same product. In this customer order table, a product is represented by its foreign key, e.g. product code, which is the primary key of the product table.

Even though the use of primary and foreign keys is not an absolute requirement for joining tables, their absence may cause you to incorrectly join tables.

Querying Multiple Tables

To query data from multiple tables, use the JOIN keyword to specify the related columns from two tables. The JOIN clause of a SELECT statement joins related rows from two or more tables, based on their primary key/foreign key relationship.

For example, a customer order (c_order) table may need a foreign key column to relate to the primary key of the product table. Additionally, the customer order table may also need a foreign key to relate to the primary key of the customer table.

The syntax for the JOIN is as follows.

```
SELECT columns FROM table_1, table_2, ... table_n
WHERE table_1.primary_key = table_2.foreign_key
AND table_2.primary_key = table_n.foregin_key;
```

To illustrate the use of joins, I will use the c_order table, customer table, and product table in Table 5.1, Table 5.2, and Table 5.3, respectively. The C_NO and P_CODE of the c_order table are foreign keys; their related primary keys are in the customer and product tables, respectively.

Use Listing 5.1 - 5.5 to create the customer table, insert four customers, create the c_order table and add six orders.

Listing 5.1: Creating customer table

```
CREATE TABLE customer
  ( c_no VARCHAR(6) NOT NULL,
    c_name VARCHAR(15),
    PRIMARY KEY (c_no) );
```

Listing 5.2: Adding customers

```
INSERT INTO customer VALUES ( 10, 'Standard Store' );
INSERT INTO customer VALUES ( 20, 'Quality Store' );
INSERT INTO customer VALUES ( 30, 'Head Office' );
INSERT INTO customer VALUES ( 40, 'Super Agent' );
```

Listing 5.3: Creating c_order table

```
CREATE TABLE c_order
  ( c_no VARCHAR(6),
    p_code VARCHAR(6),
    qty INTEGER,
    order_dt DATE,
    FOREIGN KEY (c_no) REFERENCES customer(c_no),
    FOREIGN KEY (p_code) REFERENCES product(p_code))
;
```

Listing 5.4: Adding orders

```
INSERT INTO c_order VALUES(10,1,100, '2013-4-1');
INSERT INTO c_order VALUES(10,2,100, '2013-4-1');
INSERT INTO c_order VALUES(20,1,200, '2013-4-1');
INSERT INTO c_order VALUES(30,3,300, '2013-4-2');
INSERT INTO c_order VALUES(40,4,400, '2013-4-2');
INSERT INTO c_order VALUES(40,5,400, '2013-4-3');
```

```
C_NO    P_CODE            QTY  ORDER_DT
------  ------  -----------  ----------
10      2                 100  2013-04-01
20      1                 200  2013-04-01
30      3                 300  2013-04-02
40      4                 400  2013-04-02
40      5                 400  2013-04-03
10      1                 100  2013-04-01
```

Table 5.1: The customer order (c_order) table

```
C_NO    C_NAME
------  ---------------
10      Standard Store
20      Quality Store
30      Head Office
40      Super Agent
```

Table 5.2: The customer table

```
C_NAME            P_CODE         QTY ORDER_DT
---------------   ------  ----------- ----------
Standard Store    2              100 2013-04-01
Quality Store     1              200 2013-04-01
Head Office       3              300 2013-04-02
Super Agent       4              400 2013-04-02
Super Agent       5              400 2013-04-03
Standard Store    1              100 2013-04-01
```

Table 5.3: The product table

Listing 5.5 is an example of a JOIN query. It joins the rows from the c_order table to the rows from the customer table based on the c_no foreign key column of the c_order table and the c_no primary key column of the customer table. The query returns the name of every customer who has placed one or more orders.

Listing 5.5: A two table join

```
SELECT c_name,
  p_code,
  c_order.qty,
  c_order.order_dt
FROM c_order
JOIN customer
ON c_order.c_no = customer.c_no;
```

Applied against the example c_order and customer tables, the query result is as follows.

```
C_NAME            P_CODE         QTY ORDER_DT
---------------   ------  ----------- ----------
Standard Store    2              100 2013-04-01
Quality Store     1              200 2013-04-01
Head Office       3              300 2013-04-02
Super Agent       4              400 2013-04-02
Super Agent       5              400 2013-04-03
Standard Store    1              100 2013-04-01
```

Using Table Aliases

In a join query, different tables can have columns with identical names. To make sure you refer to the correct column of a table, you need to qualify it with its table. In the previous example, c_order.c_no (the c_no column of the c_order table) and customer.c_no (the c_no column of the customer_table) were how the c_no columns were qualified. A table alias can be a more convenient (and shorter) way to qualify a column.

For example, in the query in Listing 5.2, o is an alias for the c_order table and c is an alias for the customer table. These aliases are then used in the ON clause to qualify the c_no columns with their respective tables.

Listing 5.6: Using table aliases

```
SELECT c_name,
  p_code,
  o.qty,
  o.order_dt
FROM c_order o
JOIN customer c
ON o.c_no = c.c_no;
```

Column Aliases vs. Table Aliases

In Chapter 3, "Query Output", I explained the use of aliases for columns using the AS keyword. Although a column alias can be created without using the AS keyword, its presence improves readability ("p_name AS product_name" instead of "p_name product_name"). On the other hand, table aliases cannot use the AS keyword.

Joining More than Two Tables

From the JOIN syntax presented earlier, you can join more than two tables. To do this, in the SELECT statement, join two tables at a time.

For example, the query in Listing 5.7 joins the c_order table to the customer table, and then joins the customer table to the product table. The rows in the c_order table are joined to the rows of the same c_no column from the customer table, and these rows are then joined to the rows with the same p_code from the product table. This query returns the customer names and their orders.

Listing 5.7: A three table join

```
SELECT c_name,
  p_name,
```

```
  o.qty,
  o.order_dt
FROM c_order o
JOIN customer c
ON o.c_no = c.c_no
JOIN product p
ON o.p_code = p.p_code;
```

Applied against the c_order, customer and product sample tables, you will see the following result.

```
C_NAME            P_NAME              QTY ORDER_DT
---------------   ---------------   ------------ ----------
Standard Store    Washer              100 2013-04-01
Quality Store     Nail                200 2013-04-01
Head Office       Nut                 300 2013-04-02
Super Agent       Screw               400 2013-04-02
Super Agent       Super_Nut           400 2013-04-03
Standard Store    Nail                100 2013-04-01
```

You can also apply WHERE conditions for selecting rows on a join query. For example, in Listing 5.8, thanks to the WHERE condition, only products with names that do not start with "Super" will be in the query output.

Listing 5.8: JOIN and WHERE

```
SELECT c_name,
  p_name,
  o.qty,
  o.order_dt
FROM c_order o
JOIN customer c
ON o.c_no = c.c_no
JOIN product p
ON o.p_code = p.p_code
WHERE p_name NOT LIKE 'Super%';
```

Executing the query in Listing 5.8 against the sample tables will produce the following output rows.

```
C_NAME            P_NAME              QTY ORDER_DT
---------------   ---------------   ------------ ----------
Standard Store    Washer              100 2013-04-01
Quality Store     Nail                200 2013-04-01
Head Office       Nut                 300 2013-04-02
Super Agent       Screw               400 2013-04-02
Standard Store    Nail                100 2013-04-01
```

Joining on More than One Column

The preceding joins were on one column. Tables can also be joined on more than one column.

The syntax for a multicolumn join for two tables is as follows.

```
SELECT columns FROM table_1, table_2
WHERE table_1.column_1 = table_2.column_1
AND table_1.column_2 = table_2.column_2
...
AND table_1.column_n = table_2.column_n;
```

As an example, suppose you track order shipments in the following shipment table

C_NO	P_CODE	ORDER_DT	SHIP_QTY	SHIP_DT
10	1	2013-04-01	50	2013-04-02
10	1	2013-04-01	100	2013-04-02
20	1	2013-04-01	100	2013-04-02
30	1	2013-04-02	300	2013-04-03
10	1	2013-04-01	50	2013-04-10

You can create the shipment table and insert the rows using the SQL in Listing 5.9 and 5.10.

Listing 5.9: Creating shipment table

```
CREATE TABLE shipment
  ( c_no VARCHAR(6),
    p_code VARCHAR(6),
    order_dt DATE,
    ship_qty INT,
    ship_dt DATE,
    FOREIGN KEY (c_no) REFERENCES customer(c_no),
    FOREIGN KEY (p_code) REFERENCES product(p_code));
```

Listing 5.10: Adding customers

```
INSERT INTO shipment VALUES (10,1,'2013-4-1',50,'2013-4-
    2');
INSERT INTO shipment VALUES (10,1,'2013-4-1',100,'2013-4-
    2');
INSERT INTO shipment VALUES (20,1,'2013-4-1',100,'2013-4-
    2');
INSERT INTO shipment VALUES (30,1,'2013-4-2',300,'2013-4-
    3');
INSERT INTO shipment VALUES (10,1,'2013-4-1',50,'2013-4-
    10');
```

To retrieve the order quantity (the qty column of the c_order table) of each shipment, you need to have a query that joins the shipment table to the order table on three columns, c_no, p_no, and order_dt, as shown in the query in Listing 5.11.

Listing 5.11: A multiple columns join

```
SELECT o.c_no,
   o.p_code,
   o.order_dt,
   ship_qty,
   ship_dt,
   qty
FROM shipment s
JOIN c_order o
ON s.c_no      = o.c_no
AND s.p_code   = o.p_code
AND s.order_dt = o.order_dt;
```

Executing this query against the c_order and shipment tables will give you the following output rows.

```
C_NO   P_CODE ORDER_DT       SHIP_QTY SHIP_DT
       QTY
------ ------ ---------- ------------ ---------- ----------
       --
10     1      2013-04-01           50 2013-04-02
       100
10     2      2013-04-01          100 2013-04-02
       100
20     1      2013-04-01          100 2013-04-02
       200
30     3      2013-04-02          300 2013-04-03
       300
10     1      2013-04-01           50 2013-04-10
       100
```

Outer Joins

All the joins I explained so far were inner joins. There is another type of join, the outer join. While an inner join query produces only related rows from the joined tables, an outer join query produces all rows from one table even when some of the rows do not have matching rows from the other table.

There are three subtypes of outer joins, LEFT, RIGHT, and FULL. The following points described each of these three types.

All rows from the table on the left of the left outer join will be in the output whether or not there are matching rows from the table on its right. The syntax for the left outer join is as follows.

```
SELECT columns
FROM table_1 LEFT OUTER JOIN table_2
ON table_1.column = table_2.column ... ;
```

All rows form the table on the right of the right outer join will be in the output whether or not there are matching rows from the table on its left. The syntax for the right outer join is as follows.

```
SELECT columns FROM table_1 RIGHT OUTER JOIN table_2 ON
        table_1.column = table_2.column ... ;
```

The full outer join returns all rows from both tables whether or not there are matching rows from the opposite table. The syntax for the full outer join is as follows.

```
SELECT columns
FROM table_1 FULL OUTER JOIN table_2
ON table_1.column = table_2.column … ;
```

Listing 5.12 is an example left outer join query. This query returns all rows from the c_order table.

Listing 5.12: Left outer join

```
SELECT o.*,
  ship_dt
FROM c_order o
LEFT OUTER JOIN shipment s
ON o.p_code = s.p_code
AND o.c_no  = s.c_no;
```

If you run this query against our example c_order and shipment tables, you will see the following output rows.

C_NO	P_CODE	QTY	ORDER_DT	SHIP_DT
10	1	100	2013-04-01	2013-04-02
10	2	100	2013-04-01	2013-04-02
20	1	200	2013-04-01	2013-04-02
30	3	300	2013-04-02	2013-04-03
10	1	100	2013-04-01	2013-04-10
40	5	400	2013-04-03	NULL
40	4	400	2013-04-02	NULL

Note that the last two rows have no matching rows from the shipment table and therefore their ship_dt column has NULL values.

Rows with NULL only

If you want to query only orders that have not been shipped at all, you have to put this "only" condition in the WHERE clause of your query (ship_dt IS NULL) as in the query in Listing 5.7.

Listing 5.13: NULL only rows

```
SELECT o.*,
  ship_dt
FROM c_order o
LEFT OUTER JOIN shipment s
ON o.p_code = s.p_code
AND o.c_no  = s.c_no
WHERE s.ship_dt IS NULL;
```

The following output rows from the query in Listing 5.7 are customer orders that have not been shipped.

```
C_NO    P_CODE           QTY ORDER_DT   SHIP_DT
------  ------  ----------- ---------- ----------
40      5                400 2013-04-03 NULL
40      4                400 2013-04-02 NULL
```

Full Outer Joins

Suppose any order that was canceled was deleted from the c_order table (In a real-life application, canceled orders might be moved to a different table, rather than deleted). This means, some rows of the shipment table now may not have matching rows in the order table. To return orders that do not have shipments as well shipments that do not have orders, we need to write a query with the full outer join, like the one shown in Listing 5.8.

Listing 5.14: Full outer join

```
SELECT o.*, s.ship_dt
  FROM c_order o
FULL OUTER JOIN shipment s
ON o.p_code = s.p_code
AND o.c_no  = s.c_no ;
```

To test the query, you need delete an order, such as the order(s) placed by customer 30. Our c_order table now has the following rows only. After the deletion, the c_order table has the following rows.

```
C_NO P_CODE      QTY ORDER_DT
---- ------ ---------- ---------
10   1          100 01-APR-13
```

```
10    2                 100 01-APR-13
20    1                 200 01-APR-13
40    4                 400 02-APR-13
40    5                 400 03-APR-13
```

If you run the query in Listing 5.14, you will get the following output rows. Note that we have NULL on the rows on both sides. The NULLs on the right side are from the shipment table, the NULL on the left side (in our example here we only have one row) is coming from the c_order table.

```
C_NO   P_CODE         QTY ORDER_DT   SHIP_DT
------ ------ ------------ ---------- ----------
10     2              100 2013-04-01 2013-04-02
20     1              200 2013-04-01 2013-04-02
10     1              100 2013-04-01 2013-04-02
10     1              100 2013-04-01 2013-04-10
NULL   NULL          NULL NULL       2013-04-03
40     5              400 2013-04-03 NULL
40     4              400 2013-04-02 NULL
```

Self-Joins

Assuming some of your products have substitutes and you want to record the substitutes in the product table, you then need to add a column. The new column, which is called s_code in the product table, contains the product code of the substitute.

The new product table with a row having s_code 5 now looks like the following.

```
P_CODE P_NAME           PRICE LAUNCH_DT  S_CODE
------ ---------------- ------ ---------- ------
1      Nail             10.00 2013-03-31 NULL
2      Washer           20.00 2013-03-29 NULL
3      Nut              30.00 2013-03-29 5
4      Screw            40.00 2013-03-30 NULL
5      Super_Nut        50.00 2013-03-30 NULL
6      New Nut          NULL NULL        NULL
```

To add the s_code column, execute the following statement:

```
ALTER TABLE product ADD s_code VARCHAR (6);
```

Then, to update the p_code = 3 row, execute the following statement:

```
UPDATE product SET s_code = 5 WHERE p_code = 3;
```

If you need to know the product name of a substitute, you need the query shown in Listing 5.15. This query joins the product table to itself. This kind of join is called a self-join.

The syntax for the self-join is as follows.

```
SELECT columns
FROM table alias_1
JOIN table alias_2
ON alias_1.column_x = alias_2.column_y;
```

Note that *column_x* and *column_y* are columns in the same table.

Listing 5.15: A self-join

```
SELECT prod.p_code,
  prod.p_name,
  subst.p_code subst_p_code,
  subst.p_name subst_name
FROM product prod
LEFT OUTER JOIN product subst
ON prod.s_code = subst.p_code
ORDER BY prod.p_code;
```

Here are the output rows of the query, showing "Super Nut" in the subst_name column of product 3.

P_CODE	P_NAME	SUBST_P_CODE	SUBST_NAME
1	Nail	NULL	NULL
2	Washer	NULL	NULL
3	Nut	5	Super_Nut
4	Screw	NULL	NULL
5	Super_Nut	NULL	NULL
6	New Nut	NULL	NULL

Multiple Uses of A Table

If a product can have more than one substitute, you need to store the product-substitute relationships in a separate table. A substitute cannot be recorded in the product table.

To create the table that stores the product-substitute relationships named prod_subst, execute the following statement.

```
CREATE TABLE prod_subst (p_code VARCHAR(6), s_code
    VARCHAR(6));
```

To remove the s_code column, execute the following statement:

```
ALTER TABLE product DROP (p_code);
```

Your product table will now contain the following rows.

```
P_NAME              PRICE LAUNCH_DT
--------------- ------ ----------
Nail                10.00 2013-03-31
Washer              15.00 2013-03-29
Nut                 15.00 2013-03-29
Screw               25.00 2013-03-30
Super_Nut           30.00 2013-03-30
New Nut              NULL NULL
```

Assuming that the only product with substitutes is product number 3 and its substitutes are the products number 5 and 6, the prod_subst table will have two rows as follows. (You need to insert these two rows using the INSERT statements)

```
P_CODE S_CODE
------ ------
3      5
3      6
```

To get the name of a product and the names of its substitutes, you need to use the product table twice, as shown in the query in Listing 5.16.

Listing 5.16: Multiple uses of a table

```sql
SELECT prod.p_code,
  prod.p_name,
  ps.s_code,
  subst.p_name AS s_name
FROM product prod
INNER JOIN prod_subst ps
ON prod.p_code = ps.p_code
INNER JOIN product subst
ON ps.s_code = subst.p_code
ORDER BY prod.p_code;
```

Here are the output rows from the query in Listing 5.10.

```
P_CODE P_NAME           S_CODE S_NAME
------ --------------- ------ ---------------
3      Nut              5      Super_Nut
3      Nut              6      New Nut
```

Summary

In this chapter you learned about getting data from multiple tables. You learned how to use the various types of joins for this purpose.

Chapter 6: Subqueries

A subquery is a query nested within another query. The containing query is called an outer query. A subquery in turn can have a nested query, making it a multiple nested query.

This chapter discusses subqueries in detail.

Single-Row Subqueries

A single-row subquery is a subquery that returns a single value. A single-row subquery can be placed in the WHERE clause of an outer query. The return value of the subquery is compared with a column of the outer query using one of the comparison operators. (Comparison operators were discussed in Chapter 2, "Basic Queries")

For example, the query in Listing 6.1 contains a single-row subquery that returns the highest sale price recorded for a product. The outer query returns all products from the product table that have that highest price (30.00), the Super_Nut and Newer Nut products.

Listing 6.1: A subquery that returns a single value

```
SELECT *
FROM product
WHERE price =
  (SELECT MAX(price)
  FROM product p
  INNER JOIN c_order o
  ON p.p_code = o.p_code
  );
```

Note that the subquery in Listing 6.1 is printed in bold.

Executing the query in Listing 6.1 against this product table

P_CODE	P_NAME	PRICE	LAUNCH_DT
1	Nail	10.00	2013-03-31
2	Washer	15.00	2013-03-29
3	Nut	15.00	2013-03-29
4	Screw	25.00	2013-03-30
5	Super_Nut	30.00	2013-03-30
6	Newer_Nut	30.00	2013-05-01

and the following c_order (customer order) table

C_NO	P_CODE	QTY	ORDER_DT

```
10      2               100  2013-04-01
20      1               200  2013-04-01
30      3               300  2013-04-02
40      4               400  2013-04-02
40      5               400  2013-04-03
10      1               100  2013-04-01
```

will give you the following result.

```
P_CODE  P_NAME          PRICE  LAUNCH_DT
------  --------------- ------ ----------
5       Super_Nut        30.00 2013-03-30
6       Newer_Nut        30.00 2013-05-01
```

The column and subquery result do not have to be the same column, but they must have compatible data types. In the query in Listing 6.1, the price column of the product table is a numeric type and the subquery also returns a numeric type.

If the subquery returns more than one value, you will get an error message. For example, the query in Listing 6.2 throws an error because the subquery returns more than one value.

Listing 6.2: Single-row subquery error

```
SELECT *
FROM product
WHERE price =
  (SELECT MAX(price)
  FROM product p
  INNER JOIN c_order s
  ON p.p_code = s.p_code
  GROUP BY p.launch_dt
  );
```

Here is the error that you will see if you run the query in Listing 6.2.

```
SQL0811N  The result of a scalar fullselect, SELECT INTO
      statement, or VALUES INTO statement is more than
      one row.
```

Multiple-Row Subqueries

A subquery that returns more than one value is called a multiple-row subquery. This type of subquery also occurs in the WHERE clause of an outer query, however instead of using a comparison operator, you use IN or NOT IN in the WHERE clause.

For example, the query in Listing 6.3 contains a multiple-row subquery.

Listing 6.3: Using a multiple-row subquery

```
SELECT *
FROM product
WHERE price IN
  (SELECT MAX(price)
  FROM product p
  INNER JOIN c_order s
  ON p.p_code = s.p_code
  GROUP BY p.launch_dt
  );
```

Run against the same product and order tables, the subquery will return these three values:

```
     1
------
 15.00
 30.00
 10.00
```

The overall query output will be as follows.

```
P_CODE P_NAME            PRICE LAUNCH_DT
------ ---------------- ------ ----------
1      Nail              10.00 2013-03-31
2      Washer            15.00 2013-03-29
3      Nut               15.00 2013-03-29
5      Super_Nut         30.00 2013-03-30
6      Newer_Nut         30.00 2013-05-01
```

The ALL and ANY Operators

In addition to IN and NOT IN, you can also use the ALL and ANY operators in a multiple-row subquery. With ALL or ANY you use a comparison operator. For instance, the query in Listing 6.4 uses the ALL operator to compare the price column with the subquery result.

Listing 6.4: Using ALL

```
SELECT *
FROM product
WHERE price >= ALL
  (SELECT MAX(price)
  FROM product p
  INNER JOIN c_order o
  ON p.p_code = o.p_code
  GROUP BY p.launch_dt
  )
ORDER BY p_code;
```

Run against the same product and order tables, the subquery in Listing 6.4 (printed in bold) returns these results:

```
         1
    ------
    15.00
    30.00
    10.00
```

The query output will consist of only rows whose price is greater or equal to all the values returned by the subquery.

Here is the query output.

```
P_CODE  P_NAME           PRICE  LAUNCH_DT
------  ---------------  ------ ----------
5       Super_Nut        30.00  2013-03-30
6       Newer_Nut        30.00  2013-05-01
```

As another example, the query in Listing 6.5 is similar to the one in Listing 6.4 except that the equal operator is used to compare the price with the subquery result.

Listing 6.5: Using ALL for equal comparison

```
SELECT *
FROM product
WHERE price = ALL
   (SELECT MAX(price)
   FROM product p
   INNER JOIN c_order o
   ON p.p_code = o.p_code
   GROUP BY p.launch_dt
   )
ORDER BY p_code;
```

As in the previous example, the subquery will return these values.

```
         1
    ------
    15.00
    30.00
    10.00
```

The query output then consists of only rows whose price equals to all these values, which is not possible as each product has only one price. As a result, the query returns no rows. Here is a message you will see if you run the query.

```
No rows were retrieved.
```

Subqueries Returning Rows Having the Same Value

If you use = ALL and the subquery returns one row or multiple rows with the same value you will not get a "no rows selected" message.

You can also use the ANY operator to compare a column with the values returned by a subquery. If you use ALL, the query compares a column to all values (every one of the values) returned by the subquery. If you use ANY, the query compares a column to any one of the values returned by the subquery.

For example, the query in Listing 6.6 compares the price column for equality to any of the maximum prices returned by the subquery, in other words, the WHERE condition is true if the price equals to any of maximum prices.

Listing 6.6: Using the equal comparison to ANY value

```
SELECT *
FROM product
WHERE price = ANY
  (SELECT MAX(price)
  FROM product p
  INNER JOIN c_order o
  ON p.P_code = o.p_code
  GROUP BY p.launch_dt
  )
ORDER BY p_code;
```

The subquery will return these rows.

```
     1
------
 15.00
 30.00
 10.00
```

The outer query output will consist of any product that has a price equal to any of these (maximum price) values. Here is the query output.

P_CODE	P_NAME	PRICE	LAUNCH_DT
1	Nail	10.00	2013-03-31
2	Washer	15.00	2013-03-29
3	Nut	15.00	2013-03-29
5	Super_Nut	30.00	2013-03-30
6	Newer_Nut	30.00	2013-05-01

Multiple Nested Subqueries

A subquery can contain another query, making it a query with multiple nested subqueries. The query in Listing 6.7, for example, has multiple nested subqueries. Notice the two IN's, one for each of the two nested queries? The query returns only customers who have not ordered any product having name that contains 'Nut'.

Listing 6.7: Query with multiple nested subqueries

```
SELECT customer.*
FROM customer
WHERE c_no IN
  (SELECT c_no
  FROM c_order
  WHERE p_code IN
    (SELECT p_code FROM product WHERE p_name NOT LIKE
      '%Nut%'
    )
  );
```

Here is the query result.

```
C_NO    C_NAME
------  ---------------
10      Standard Store
20      Quality Store
40      Super Agent
```

Correlated Subqueries

All the preceding subqueries are independent of their outer queries. A subquery can also be related to its outer query, where one or more column from the outer query table is (are) related to the column(s) of the subquery table in the WHERE clause of the subquery. This type of subquery is called the correlated subquery.

As an example, the query in Listing 6.8 contains a correlated subquery that returns only customers who have not ordered any product whose name contains 'Nut'. Note that the c_no column of the outer query table, customer, is related to the c_no column of the c_order table of the subquery.

Listing 6.8: Using a correlated subquery

```
SELECT customer.*
FROM customer
WHERE c_no IN
  (SELECT c_no
```

```
FROM c_order o
JOIN product p
ON o.p_code = p.p_code
WHERE p_name NOT LIKE '%Nut%'
AND customer.c_no = o.c_no
);
```

The following are the query result.

```
C_NO    C_NAME
------  ---------------
10      Standard Store
20      Quality Store
40      Super Agent
```

Summary

In this chapter you learned the various types of subqueries, such as nested and correlated subqueries. In the next chapters you will apply the lesson you learned in this chapter to combine the results of two or more queries.

Chapter 7: Compound Queries

You can combine the results of two or more SELECT statements using the UNION ALL, UNION, INTERSECT, or MINUS operators. The number of output columns from every statement must be the same and the corresponding columns must have identical or compatible data types.

This chapter shows you how to combine query results.

UNION ALL

When you combine two or more queries with the UNION ALL operator, the overall output will be the total rows from all the queries. For example, take a look at the query in Listing 7.1. This query consists of two SELECT statements.

Listing 7.1: Using UNION ALL

```
SELECT p_code, p_name, 'FIRST QUERY' query
FROM product p WHERE p_name LIKE '%Nut%'
UNION ALL
SELECT p.p_code,
  p_name,
  'SECOND_QUERY' query
FROM c_order o
INNER JOIN product p
ON o.p_code = p.p_code;
```

Note that the 'FIRST QUERY' and 'SECOND_QUERY' literals in the first and second SELECT statements, respectively, are just labels to identify where a row is coming from.

Assuming that the product table has the following rows

P_CODE	P_NAME	PRICE	LAUNCH_DT
1	Nail	10	31-MAR-13
2	Washer	15	29-MAR-13
3	Nut	15	29-MAR-13
4	Screw	25	30-MAR-13
5	Super_Nut	30	30-MAR-13
6	New Nut	30	01-MAY-13

and the c_order table contains the following records

C_NO	P_CODE	QTY	ORDER_DT
10	1	100	01-APR-13

```
10    2         100  01-APR-13
20    1         200  01-APR-13
40    4         400  02-APR-13
40    5         400  03-APR-13
30    3         300  02-APR-13
```

the query in Listing 7.1 will return the following output.

```
P_CODE  P_NAME       QUERY
------  ----------   ------------
3       Nut          FIRST QUERY
5       Super_Nut    FIRST QUERY
6       New Nut      FIRST QUERY
1       Nail         SECOND_QUERY
1       Nail         SECOND_QUERY
2       Washer       SECOND_QUERY
3       Nut          SECOND_QUERY
4       Screw        SECOND_QUERY
5       Super_Nut    SECOND_QUERY
```

Note that the output of the query in Listing 7.1 comprises all the records form the first SELECT statement followed by the rows from the second SELECT statement. You can of course use the ORDER BY clause to re-order this. For instance, the query in Listing 7.2 modifies the query in Listing 7.1 by ordering the results on the p_code column using the ORDER BY clause.

Listing 7.2: Ordering output rows of a compound query

```
SELECT p_code, p_name, 'FIRST QUERY' query
FROM product p WHERE p_name LIKE '%Nut%'
UNION ALL
SELECT p.p_code,
   p_name,
   'SECOND_QUERY' query
FROM c_order o
INNER JOIN product p
ON o.p_code = p.p_code
ORDER BY p_code;
```

The result of the query in Listing 7.2 is as follows.

```
P_CODE  P_NAME       QUERY
------  ----------   ------------
1       Nail         SECOND_QUERY
1       Nail         SECOND_QUERY
2       Washer       SECOND_QUERY
3       Nut          SECOND_QUERY
3       Nut          FIRST QUERY
4       Screw        SECOND_QUERY
```

```
5        Super_Nut   SECOND_QUERY
5        Super_Nut   FIRST QUERY
6        New Nut     FIRST QUERY
```

UNION

UNION is similar to UNION ALL. However, with UNION duplicate rows will be returned once only. For example, consider the query in Listing 7.3 that consists of two SELECT elements.

Listing 7.3: Using UNION

```
SELECT p_code,
  p_name
FROM product p
WHERE p_name LIKE '%Nut%'
UNION
SELECT p.p_code,
  p_name
FROM c_order o
INNER JOIN product p
ON o.p_code = p.p_code
ORDER BY p_code;
```

Here is the output of the query.

```
P_CODE P_NAME
------ ----------
1      Nail
2      Washer
3      Nut
4      Screw
5      Super_Nut
6      New Nut
```

INTERSECT

When you combine two or more queries with the INTERSECT operator, the output will consist of rows common to all the participating SELECT statements. In other words, only if a row is returned by all the SELECT statements will the row be included in the final result.

Let's take a look at the example in Listing 7.4.

Listing 7.4: Using INTERSECT

```
SELECT p_code,
  p_name
FROM product p
WHERE p_name LIKE '%Nut%'
```

```
INTERSECT
SELECT p.p_code,
  p_name
FROM c_order o
INNER JOIN product p
ON o.p_code = p.p_code
ORDER BY p_code;
```

Running the query against the same product and c_order tables will return the following result.

```
P_CODE P_NAME
------ ---------
3      Nut
5      Super_Nut
```

MINUS

When you combine two SELECT statements using the MINUS operator, the final output will be rows from the first query that are not returned by the second query. Take a look at the example in Listing 7.5.

Listing 7.5: Using MINUS

```
SELECT p_code,
  p_name
FROM product p
WHERE p_name LIKE '%Nut%'
MINUS
SELECT p.p_code,
  p_name
FROM c_order o
INNER JOIN product p
ON o.p_code = p.p_code
ORDER BY p_code;
```

Running this query against the same product and c_order tables produces the following output.

```
P_CODE P_NAME
------ ---------
6      New Nut
```

With MINUS, the order of constituting SELECT statements is important. If you swap the two SELECT statements in the query in Listing 7.5, the output will be totally different. Take a look at the query in Listing 7.6, which is identical to that in Listing 7.5 except for the fact that the two SELECT statements have been swapped.

Listing 7.6: Swapping the participating SELECT statements in a query combined with MINUS

```
SELECT p.p_code,
  p_name
FROM c_order o
INNER JOIN product p
ON o.p_code = p.p_code
MINUS
SELECT p_code,
  p_name
FROM product p
WHERE p_name LIKE '%Nut%'
ORDER BY p_code;
```

The output of the query in Listing 7.6 is this:

```
P_CODE  P_NAME
------  ------
1       Nail
2       Washer
4       Screw
```

Note that you can substitute MINUS with EXCEPT, as they are equivalent.

Summary

In this chapter you learned that you can combine the output of two or more SELECT statements. There are five operators you can use for this purpose, UNION ALL, UNION, INTERSECT, and MINUS.

Chapter 8: Views

A view is effectively a predefined query. You create and use views most frequently for the following purposes:

- Hiding table columns (for security protection)
- Presenting pre-computed columns (in lieu of table columns)
- Hiding queries (so that the query outputs are available without running the queries)

This chapter discusses view and presents examples of views.

Creating and Using Views

You create a view using the CREATE VIEW statement. Here is its syntax.

```
CREATE VIEW view_name (columns) AS SELECT ... ;
```

The SELECT statement at the end of the CREATE VIEW statement is the predefined query. When you use a view its predefined query is executed. Since a query result is a table that is not persisted (stored) in the database, a view is also known as a virtual table. The table in the SELECT statement of a view is known as a base table.

One of the reasons you use a view is when you have a table you need to share with other people. If you don't want some of the table columns viewable by others, you can use a view to hide those columns. You would then share the view and restrict access to the base table.

For example, Listing 8.1 shows an SQL statement for creating a view called product_v that is based on the product table. The view hides the price column of the base table.

Listing 8.1: Using a view to hide columns

```
CREATE VIEW product_v
  (p_code , p_name
  ) AS
SELECT p_code, p_name FROM product;
```

The product_v view can now be used just as you would any database table. For example, the following statement displays all columns in the product_v view.

```
SELECT * FROM product_v WHERE p_name NOT LIKE '%Nut%';
```

Assuming the product table contains these rows

```
P_CODE  P_NAME            PRICE  LAUNCH_DT
------  ---------------   -----  ----------
1       Nail              10.00  2013-03-31
2       Washer            15.00  2013-03-29
3       Nut               15.00  2013-03-29
4       Screw             25.00  2013-03-30
5       Super_Nut         30.00  2013-03-30
6       New Nut           NULL   NULL
```

The query returns these rows.

```
P_CODE  P_NAME
------  ---------------
1       Nail
2       Washer
4       Screw
```

Note that within a database a view name must be unique among all the views and tables in the database.

Another use of the view is to derive computed columns not available in the base table(s). Here is an example.

Suppose the product table stores profit margins for each product as follows.

```
P_CODE  P_NAME            PRICE  LAUNCH_DT   MARGIN
------  ---------------   -----  ----------  ------
1       Nail              10.00  2013-03-31       1
2       Washer            15.00  2013-03-29       2
3       Nut               15.00  2013-03-29       2
4       Screw             25.00  2013-03-30       5
5       Super_Nut         30.00  2013-03-30       5
6       New Nut           NULL   NULL          NULL
```

If you want other users to see the selling price (price + margin) but not the supplier price (price) or the margins in the product table, you can create a view that computes the selling price from the product price and margin, as demonstrated by the query in Listing 8.2. This query creates a view called product_sell_v that includes a computed column sell_price. The value for sell_price comes from the price and margin columns in the product table.

Listing 8.2: A view with a computed column

```
CREATE VIEW product_sell_v
   (p_no , p_name, sell_price
   ) AS
SELECT p_code, p_name, (price + margin) FROM product;
```

Selecting all data from product_sell_v (using "SELECT * FROM product_sell_v") returns these rows.

```
P_NO   P_NAME            SELL_PRICE
------ ----------------  ----------
1      Nail                   11.00
2      Washer                 17.00
3      Nut                    17.00
4      Screw                  30.00
5      Super_Nut              35.00
6      New Nut                 NULL
```

Users of a view don't need to know the details of its predefined query. They only need to know what data is available from the view. Referring back to the self-join example in Chapter 6, "Joins", you can create the view defined in Listing 8.3 to hide the self-join query. While the rows from the product table only have the product code of the substitutes, this view will give you the names of their substitutes as well.

Listing 8.3: Hiding Query

```
CREATE VIEW prod_subs_v AS
SELECT prod.p_code,
  prod.p_name,
  subst.p_code subst_p_code,
  subst.p_name subst_name
FROM product prod
LEFT OUTER JOIN product subst
ON prod.s_code = subst.p_code
;
```

Recall that the product table has the following rows.

```
P_CODE P_NAME            PRICE LAUNCH_DT   MARGIN S_CODE
------ ----------------  ----- ----------  ------ ------
1      Nail              10.00 2013-03-31       1 6
2      Washer            15.00 2013-03-29       2 NULL
3      Nut               15.00 2013-03-29       2 5
4      Screw             25.00 2013-03-30       5 NULL
5      Super_Nut         30.00 2013-03-30       5 NULL
6      New Nut           NULL  NULL          NULL NULL
```

Executing the following query that uses the view created with the statement in Listing 8.3,

```
SELECT * FROM prod_subs_v;
```

produces the following rows.

```
P_CODE P_NAME            SUBST_P_CODE SUBST_NAME
------ ----------------  ------------ ----------------
3      Nut               5            Super_Nut
```

```
1        Nail            6           New Nut
2        Washer          NULL        NULL
4        Screw           NULL        NULL
5        Super_Nut       NULL        NULL
6        New Nut         NULL        NULL
```

Nested Views

A view can be based on another view. Such a view is called a nested view.

As an example, the ps_noname_v view in Listing 8.4 hides the p_name column and is based on the product_sell_v view created earlier.

Listing 8.4: A nested view

```
CREATE VIEW ps_noname_v
   (p_no , sell_price
   ) AS
SELECT p_no, sell_price FROM product_sell_v;
```

Running this statement

```
SELECT * FROM ps_noname_v;
```

will give you the following output rows

```
P_NO    SELL_PRICE
------  -----------
1           11.00
2           17.00
3           17.00
4           30.00
5           35.00
6            NULL
```

Managing Views

You can easily manage your views in DB2. To see all views in the current database, execute the following statement.

```
 SELECT tabname FROM SYSCAT.TABLES
WHERE type = 'V' AND owner = 'DJONI';
```

This will return the following output, which may differ for other databases.

```
TABNAME
--------------
PRODUCT_V
PRODUCT_SELL_V
PROD_SUBS_V
```

```
PS_NONAME_V
```

Note that SYSCAT.TABLES is a view in the DB2 catalog; you will learn about the catalog in Chapter 11, "Catalog".

To delete a view, use the DROP VIEW statement. The syntax for the DROP VIEW statement is as follows.

```
DROP VIEW view_name;
```

For example, the statement in Listing 8.5 will delete the ps_noname_v view.

Listing 8.5: Deleting the ps_noname_v view

```
DROP VIEW ps_noname_v;
```

After running the statement in Listing 9.5, listing the views in the database again will give you these results.

```
TABNAME
--------------
PRODUCT_V
PRODUCT_SELL_V
PROD_SUBS_V
```

Summary

A view is a predefined query that you can use to hide columns, include pre-computed columns, and so on. In this chapter you learned how to create and manage views.

Chapter 9: Built-in Functions

The DB2 database provides functions that you can use in your queries. These built-in functions can be grouped into numeric functions, character functions, datetime functions, and functions for handling null values. The objective of this chapter is to introduce you to some of these functions.

Numeric Functions

The following are some of the more important numeric functions.

ABS

ABS(n) returns the absolute value of n. For example, the following query returns the absolute value of (price - 20.00) as the third column.

```
SELECT p_code, price, price - 20 "price-20", ABS(price -
    20.00) "ABS(price-20)" FROM product;
```

Applying the query to this product table

P_CODE	P_NAME	PRICE	LAUNCH_DT	MARGIN
1	Nail	10.00	2013-03-31	1
2	Washer	15.00	2013-03-29	2
3	Nut	15.00	2013-03-29	2
4	Screw	25.00	2013-03-30	5
5	Super_Nut	30.00	2013-03-30	5
6	New Nut	NULL	NULL	NULL

you will get this result.

P_CODE	PRICE	PRICE-20	ABS(PRICE-20)
1	10.00	-10.00	10.00
2	15.00	-5.00	5.00
3	15.00	-5.00	5.00
4	25.00	5.00	5.00
5	30.00	10.00	10.00
6	30.00	10.00	10.00

ROUND

ROUND(*n*, *d*) returns a number rounded to a certain number of decimal places. The argument *n* is the number to be rounded and *d* the number of decimal places. For example, the following query uses ROUND to round price to one decimal place.

```
SELECT p_code, price, ROUND (price, 1) FROM product;
```

Assuming the product table contains these rows

P_CODE	P_NAME	PRICE	LAUNCH_DT_
1	Nail	10.15	2013-03-31
2	Washer	15.99	2013-03-29
3	Nut	15.50	2013-03-29
4	Screw	25.25	2013-03-30
5	Super_Nut	30.33	2013-03-30
6	New Nut	NULL	NULL

the output of the query is this.

P_CODE	PRICE	ROUND(PRICE,1)
1	10.15	10.20
2	15.99	16.00
3	15.50	15.50
4	25.25	25.30
5	30.33	30.30
6	NULL	NULL

SIGN

SIGN(*n*) returns a value indicating the sign of n. This function returns -1 for *n* < 0, 0 for *n* = 0, and 1 for *n* > 0. As an example, the following query uses SIGN to return the sign of (price − 15).

```
SELECT p_code, price, SIGN(price - 15) FROM product;
```

Assuming the product table has the following records

P_CODE	P_NAME	PRICE	LAUNCH_DT
1	Nail	10.00	2013-03-31
2	Washer	15.00	2013-03-29
3	Nut	15.00	2013-03-29
4	Screw	25.00	2013-03-30
5	Super_Nut	30.00	2013-03-30
6	New Nut	NULL	NULL

the query output will be as follows.

```
P_CODE   PRICE                              SIGN
------   ------   ---------------------   ------
1        10.00                              -1.0
2        15.00                               0.0
3        15.00                               0.0
4        25.00                               1.0
5        30.00                               1.0
6         NULL                              NULL
```

TRUNC

TRUNC(n, d) returns a number truncated to a certain number of decimal places. The argument n is the number to truncate and d the number of decimal places. For example, the following query truncates price to one decimal place.

```
SELECT p_code, price, TRUNCATE(price, 1) FROM product;
```

Assuming the product table contains these rows

```
P_CODE   P_NAME            PRICE   LAUNCH_DT
------   ---------------   ------  ----------
1        Nail              10.15   2013-03-31
2        Washer            15.99   2013-03-29
3        Nut               15.50   2013-03-29
4        Screw             25.25   2013-03-30
5        Super_Nut         30.33   2013-03-30
6        New Nut            NULL   NULL
```

the query result will be as follows.

```
P_CODE   PRICE   TRUNC(PRICE,1)
------   ------  ---------------
1        10.15       10.10
2        15.99       15.90
3        15.50       15.50
4        25.25       25.20
5        30.33       30.30
6         NULL        NULL
```

Character Functions

The following are some of the more important string functions.

CONCAT

CONCAT(*string1*, *string2*) concatenates *string1* and *string2* and returns the result. If you pass a number as an argument, the number will first be converted to a string. In the following example three strings, *p_name*, a dash, and *description*, are concatenated.

```
SELECT p_code, CONCAT(CONCAT(p_name, ' -- ') , price)
    FROM product;
```

The price column value will be converted automatically to a string.

   With the product table containing these rows

```
P_CODE P_NAME           PRICE  LAUNCH_DT
------ --------------- ------ ----------
1      Nail             10.15 2013-03-31
2      Washer           15.99 2013-03-29
3      Nut              15.50 2013-03-29
4      Screw            25.25 2013-03-30
5      Super_Nut        30.33 2013-03-30
6      New Nut           NULL NULL
```

executing the query against the product table will return this result.

```
P_CODE CONCAT
------ ------------------------
1      Nail -- 10.15
2      Washer -- 15.99
3      Nut -- 15.50
4      Screw -- 25.25
5      Super_Nut -- 30.33
6      NULL
```

You can also use the || operator to concatenate strings. The following query produces the same output as the one above.

```
SELECT p_code, p_name || ' -- ' || price FROM product;
```

LOWER and UPPER

LOWER(*str*) converts *str* to lowercase and UPPER(*str*) converts *str* to uppercase. For example, the following query uses LOWER and UPPER.

```
SELECT p_name, LOWER(p_name) "lower", UPPER(p_name)
    "UPPER" FROM product;
```

Executing the query against the product table gives you this result.

```
P_NAME          2               3
--------------- --------------- ---------------
Nail            nail            NAIL
```

```
Washer          washer          WASHER
Nut             nut             NUT
Screw           screw           SCREW
Super_Nut       super_nut       SUPER_NUT
New Nut         new nut         NEW NUT
```

LENGTH

LENGTH(*str*) returns the length of string *str*. The length of a string is the number of characters in it. For example, the following query returns the length of p_name as the second column.

```
SELECT p_name, LENGTH(p_name) FROM product;
```

The result would look like this.

```
P_NAME                  LENGTH
--------------- -----------
Nail                         4
Washer                       6
Nut                          3
Screw                        5
Super_Nut                    9
New Nut                      7
```

SUBSTR

SUBSTR(*str*, *start_position*, [*length*]) returns a substring of *str* starting from the position indicated by *start_position*. If *length* is not specified, the function returns a substring from *start_position* to the last character in *str*. If *length* is present, the function returns a substring which is *length* characters long starting from *start_position*. If *length* is less than 1, the function returns an empty string.

Suppose you have a customer table with the following rows.

```
C_NO   C_NAME          PHONE
------ --------------- ----------------
10     Standard Store  1-416-223-4455
20     Quality Store   1-647-333-5566
30     Head Office     1-416-111-2222
40     Super Agent     1-226-777-8888
```

The following query

```
SELECT SUBSTR(phone, 3) "SUBSTR" FROM customer;
```

will return the following result

```
SUBSTR(PHONE,3)
---------------
416-223-4455
647-333-5566
416-111-2222
226-777-8888
```

And the following query

```
SELECT CONCAT( SUBSTR(phone, 7, 3) , SUBSTR(phone, 11,
     3)) phone
FROM customer;
```

will return this result.

```
PHONE
------
223445
333556
111222
777888
```

Datetime Functions

The following are some of the more important datetime functions.

CURRENT_DATE

CURRENT_DATE() returns the current date (the current date of the MySQL server at the time you run the query). For instance, the following query

```
SELECT p_code, launch_dt, CURRENT_DATE FROM product;
```

will return a result that looks like this. The actual value of the third column will depend on when you run the query.

```
P_CODE LAUNCH_DT  CURRENT_DATE
------ ---------- ------------
1      2013-03-31 2014-07-15
2      2013-03-29 2014-07-15
3      2013-03-29 2014-07-15
4      2013-03-30 2014-07-15
5      2013-03-30 2014-07-15
6      NULL       2014-07-15
```

VARCHAR_FORMAT

VARCHAR_FORMAT(*dt*, *fmt_specifier*) converts a date (*dt*) to a string in the format specified by *fmt_specifier*. In the following example, the launch_dt column is formatted with a format specifier that has three components:

- DD - the day of the month
- MM - the long name of the month
- YYYY - the year

```
SELECT p_code, VARCHAR_FORMAT(launch_dt, 'DD MM YYYY')
     reformatted_dt
FROM product;
```

Running the query will give you something like this.

```
P_CODE REFORMATTED_DT
------ --------------
1       31 MAR 2013
2       29 MAR 2013
3       29 MAR 2013
4       30 MAR 2013
5       30 MAR 2013
6       NULL
```

NULL-related functions

The following are some of the functions that can be used to handle null values.

COALESCE

COALESCE(*expr-1*, *expr-2*, ..., *expr-n*) returns the first expression from the list that is not NULL. For example, suppose your product table contains the following rows

```
P_CODE P_NAME          PRICE LAUNCH_DT  MIN_PRICE
------ --------------- ------ ---------- ---------
1      Nail             10.15 2013-03-31     NULL
2      Washer           15.99 2013-03-29     NULL
3      Nut              15.50 2013-03-29    12.00
4      Screw            25.25 2013-03-30    17.00
5      Super_Nut         NULL 2013-03-30    10.00
6      New Nut           NULL NULL          NULL
```

and you want to view the sale_price column of the products using this formula:

- If price is available (not NULL) then discount it by 10%

- If price is not available then return min_price
- If both price and min_price are not available, return 5.0

You can use COALESCE to produce the correct sale_price values:

```
SELECT p_name, price, min_price,
COALESCE((price * 0.9), min_price, 5.0) sale_price
FROM product;
```

Here is the query result.

P_NAME	PRICE	MIN_PRICE	SALE_PRICE
Nail	10.15	NULL	9.135
Washer	15.99	NULL	14.391
Nut	15.50	12.00	13.950
Screw	25.25	17.00	22.725
Super_Nut	NULL	10.00	10.000
New Nut	NULL	NULL	5.000

NULLIF

NULLIF (*expr1*, *expr2*) compares *expr1* and *expr2*. If they are equal, the function returns null. If they are not equal, the function returns *expr1*.

Suppose you store product old prices in a table named old_price. The following old_price table, for example, shows two old prices of the Nut product, the products with p_code = 3.

```
+--------+-----------+-------+------------+
| p_code | p_name    | price | launch_dt  |
+--------+-----------+-------+------------+
| 3      | Nut       | 15.00 | 2013-03-01 |
| 3      | Newer Nut | 12.00 | 2013-04-01 |
+--------+-----------+-------+------------+
```

Just say you want to show the old products with their current price. The following query that employs the NULLIF function can solve your problem.

```
SELECT p.p_code,
  p.p_name,
  NULLIF(p.price, op.price) current_price
FROM product p
JOIN old_price op on p.p_code=op.p_code;
```

Applying the query against the following product table and the old_price table

```
P_CODE P_NAME              PRICE LAUNCH_DT  MIN_PRICE
------ ---------------     ----- ---------- ---------
1      Nail                10.15 2013-03-31      NULL
2      Washer              15.99 2013-03-29      NULL
3      Nut                 15.50 2013-03-29     12.00
4      Screw               25.25 2013-03-30     17.00
5      Super_Nut            NULL 2013-03-30     10.00
6      New Nut              NULL NULL            NULL
```

returns the two old nuts as follows

```
P_CODE P_NAME              CURRENT_PRICE
------ ---------------     --------------
3      Nut                         15.50
3      Nut                         15.50
```

NVL2

NVL2(*expr1*, *expr2*, *expr3*) returns *exprs2* if *expr1* is not NULL; otherwise, it returns *expr3*.

For example, suppose you want to compare old and current prices. Applying NVL2 in the following query gives you NULL on the old price if the product has been superseded; otherwise, if a product has been superseded (p_code 3), its old price will come from the old_product table.

```
SELECT p.p_code,
  p.p_name,
  p.price current_price,
  NVL2(op.price,op.price,NULL) old_price
FROM product p
LEFT OUTER JOIN old_price op ON p.p_code = op.p_code;
```

Here is the result.

```
P_CODE P_NAME              CURRENT_PRICE OLD_PRICE
------ ---------------     -------------- ---------
3      Nut                         15.50     15.00
3      Nut                         15.50     12.00
4      Screw                       25.25      NULL
1      Nail                        10.15      NULL
6      New Nut                      NULL      NULL
2      Washer                      15.99      NULL
5      Super_Nut                    NULL      NULL
```

The query result shows that the only product that has been superseded is Nut, and it has been superseded twice. Therefore, its old prices are shown from the old_product table. The other products have never been superseded so their current and old prices are the same. Their old_price is coming from the product table because its op.price column, the first parameter of the NVL function, is NULL.

Summary

You learned some of the built-in functions that you can use in the MySQL database. If you are interested in learning more about built-in functions, consult the DB2 manual, available at IBM website.

Chapter 10: PL/SQL

PL/SQL, short for Procedural Language extension to SQL, complements SQL with a procedural programming language.

The objective of this chapter is to introduce some of the most commonly used PL/SQL features such as

- row-by-row processing of query output
- if-then-else decision logic
- exception handling
- stored program

Setting up DB2 for PL/SQL

PL/SQL, used to be available only in the Oracle database, is currently supported in DB2; but, you must set DB2 to enable its PL/SQL as follows.

Close your CLPPlus, then start the DB2 Command Window – Administrator from the Windows start menu.

When prompted to confirm that the program is allowed to make changes to your computer, click Yes.

On the Administrator window, run the three commands as shown.

```
Administrator: DB2 CLP - DB2COPY1                    _ □ ×

D:\DB2\BIN>db2set db2_compatibility_vector=ora

D:\DB2\BIN>db2stop
SQL1064N  DB2STOP processing was successful.

D:\DB2\BIN>db2start
SQL1063N  DB2START processing was successful.

D:\DB2\BIN>
```

Your DB2 is now set to compile and run PL/SQL programs.

Row-by-row Processing

You learned in the previous chapters that the output of a query can be more than one row. You can write a PL/SQL program to process query output row-by-row sequentially.

The structure of the PL/SQL program for row-by-row processing is as follows.

```
BEGIN
  FOR output_row_variable IN (
    SELECT ...)
  LOOP
    row processing statements;
  END LOOP;
END;
```

For example, the program in Listing 10.1 makes use of a join query and its output rows are stored in a variable named *invc*. In the processing loop, every row from *invc* is inserted into the invoice table.

Listing 10.1: Row-by-row processing

```
BEGIN
  FOR invc IN
  (SELECT c.c_no,
    c_name,
    p_name,
    qty,
    price unit_prc,
    (qty * price) total_prc,
    sysdate invoice_dt,
    launch_dt
  FROM c_order co
```

```
    JOIN product p   on co.p_code=p.p_code
    JOIN customer c on co.c_no=c.c_no
    )
    LOOP
        INSERT
        INTO invoice VALUES
          (
            invc.c_no,
            invc.c_name,
            invc.p_name,
            invc.qty,
            invc.unit_prc,
            invc.total_prc,
            invc.invoice_dt
          );
      END LOOP;
END;
```

Suppose you have c_order, customer, and product tables like the ones shown in Tables 10.1, 10.2, and 10.3, respectively, and suppose you also have an invoice table that is empty.

```
C_NO P_CODE        QTY ORDER_DT
---- ------ ----------- ----------
10   1          10 2013-04-01
10   2          10 2013-04-01
20   1          20 2013-04-01
30   3          30 2013-04-02
40   4          40 2013-04-02
40   5          40 2013-04-03
```

Table 10.1: The c_order table

```
C_NO C_NAME
---- ---------------
10   Standard Store
20   Quality Store
30   Head Office
40   Super Agent
```

Table 10.2: The customer table

```
P_CODE P_NAME     PRICE LAUNCH_DT
------ ---------- ------ ----------
1      Nail       10.00 2013-03-31
2      Washer     15.00 2013-03-29
3      Nut        15.00 2013-03-29
4      Screw      25.00 2013-03-30
5      Super_Nut  30.00 2013-03-30
6      New Nut     NULL NULL
6      New Nut    NULL   NULL
```

Table 10.3: The product table

Use the following SQL's to create the tables and insert their rows.

Listing 5.1: Creating customer table

```
CREATE TABLE customer
  ( c_no VARCHAR(6) NOT NULL,
    c_name VARCHAR(15),
    PRIMARY KEY (c_no) );
```

Listing 5.2: Adding customers

```
INSERT INTO customer VALUES ( 10, 'Standard Store');
INSERT INTO customer VALUES ( 20, 'Quality Store' );
INSERT INTO customer VALUES ( 30, 'Head Office' );
INSERT INTO customer VALUES ( 40, 'Super Agent' );
```

Listing 5.3: Creating c_order table

```
CREATE TABLE c_order
  ( c_no VARCHAR(6),
    p_code VARCHAR(6),
    qty INTEGER,
    order_dt DATE,
    FOREIGN KEY (c_no) REFERENCES customer(c_no),
    FOREIGN KEY (p_code) REFERENCES product(p_code))
;
```

Listing 5.4: Adding orders

```
INSERT INTO c_order VALUES(10,1,100, '2013-4-1');
INSERT INTO c_order VALUES(10,2,100, '2013-4-1');
INSERT INTO c_order VALUES(20,1,200, '2013-4-1');
INSERT INTO c_order VALUES(30,3,300, '2013-4-2');
INSERT INTO c_order VALUES(40,4,400, '2013-4-2');
INSERT INTO c_order VALUES(40,5,400, '2013-4-3');

CREATE TABLE invoice (   c_no VARCHAR(6),
         c_name VARCHAR (15),
         p_name VARCHAR (15),
         qty INTEGER,
         unit_prc DECIMAL(4,2),
         total_prc DECIMAL (10,2),
         invoice_dt DATE);
```

If you enter and execute the PL/SQL program in Listing 10.1 in SQL*Plus, your SQL*Plus screen will look like that in Figure 10.1. Note that to execute a PL/SQL program you need to enter the forward slash / after the last END;.

```
CLPPlus                                                    _ □ ×
SQL> BEGIN
   2     FOR invc IN
   3     (SELECT c.c_no,
   4       c_name,
   5       p_name,
   6       qty,
   7       price unit_prc,
   8       (qty * price) total_prc,
   9       sysdate invoice_dt,
  10       launch_dt
  11     FROM c_order co
  12     JOIN product p on co.p_code=p.p_code
  13     JOIN customer c on co.c_no=c.c_no
  14     )
  15     LOOP
  16        INSERT
  17        INTO invoice VALUES
  18          (
  19            invc.c_no,
  20            invc.c_name,
  21            invc.p_name,
  22            invc.qty,
  23            invc.unit_prc,
  24            invc.total_prc,
  25            invc.invoice_dt
  26          );
  27      END LOOP;
  28 END;
  29 /

DB250000I: The command completed successfully.

SQL>
```

Figure 10.1: Executing PL/SQL program in SQL*Plus

After the program is executed, the invoice table will be populated with
the following rows.

C_NO	C_NAME	P_NAME	QTY	UNIT_PRC	TOTAL_PRC	INVOICE_DT
10	Standard Store	Nail	10	10.00	100.00	2014-07-20
20	Quality Store	Nail	20	10.00	200.00	2014-07-20
10	Standard Store	Washer	10	15.00	150.00	2014-07-20
30	Head Office	Nut	30	15.00	450.00	2014-07-20
40	Super Agent	Screw	40	25.00	1000.00	2014-07-20
40	Super Agent	Super_Nut	40	30.00	1200.00	2014-07-20

If-Then-Else Decision Logic

You can use an if statement to branch in a program. For instance, the if-then-else decision logic in Listing 10.2 treats the output rows differently based on the product launch_dt.

Listing 10.2: If-then-else decision logic

```
BEGIN
  FOR invc IN
  (SELECT c_no,
    c_name,
    p_name,
    qty,
    price unit_prc,
    (qty * price) total_prc,
    sysdate invoice_dt,
    launch_dt
  FROM c_order co  JOIN product p ON co.p_code = p.p_code
  JOIN customer c ON co.c_no = c.c_no
  )
  LOOP
    IF invc.launch_dt IS NOT NULL THEN
      INSERT
      INTO invoice VALUES
        (
          invc.c_no,
          invc.c_name,
          invc.p_name,
          invc.qty,
          invc.unit_prc,
          invc.total_prc,
          invc.invoice_dt
        );
    ELSE
      NULL;
    END IF;
  END LOOP;
END;
```

For this example, I'm using a c_order table with the following rows. The difference between this c_order table and the one used in the previous example is this table has a sixth row that records the sale of a product (p_co = 6) with a null launch_dt.

```
C_NO P_CO  QTY ORDER_DT
---- ---- ---- ---------
10   1     100 01-APR-13
10   2     100 01-APR-13
20   1     200 01-APR-13
```

```
40    4      400 02-APR-13
40    5      400 03-APR-13
40    6      600 01-MAY-13
```

Because the product's launch_dt is NULL, the process does not insert an invoice row for this additional order. If you execute the program in Listing 10.2, the same rows as in the previous example will be inserted into the invoice table.

Exception Handling

PL/SQL allows you to handle errors (or exceptions) in your program using the EXCEPTION statement. Its syntax is as follows.

```
EXCEPTION
WHEN exception_name
THEN exception_handling_statement;
```

For example, suppose you want to query a specific invoice from an invoice table using the PL/SQL program in Listing 10.3. The SELECT INTO query in Listing 10.3 stores its output rows into an invc variable, which is declared to have a ROWTYPE data type.

Listing 10.3: PL/SQL program without exception handling

```
DECLARE
  invc invoice%ROWTYPE;
BEGIN
  SELECT *
  INTO invc
  FROM invoice
  WHERE c_no = '&c_no_prompt'
  AND p_name = '&p_name_prompt'
  AND TO_CHAR(invoice_dt, 'DD-MON-YY') =
      '&invoice_dt_prompt';
  dbms_output.put_line(invc.c_name || ' - ' ||
      invc.p_name || ' - ' || invc.total_prc);
END;
```

The PL/SQL program in Listing 10.3 has a dbm_output.put_line procedure to display its characters string parameter. You need to issue a SET SERVEROUTPUT ON to enable the output display of the procedure.

```
SQL> set serveroutput on
SQL>
```

Assume the invoice table has the following rows.

C_NO	C_NAME	P_NAME	QTY	UNIT_PRC	TOTAL_PRC	INVOICE_DT
10	Standard Store	Nail	10	10.00	100.00	2014-07-20
20	Quality Store	Nail	20	10.00	200.00	2014-07-20
10	Standard Store	Washer	10	15.00	150.00	2014-07-20
40	Super Agent	Screw	40	25.00	1000.00	2014-07-20
40	Super Agent	Super_Nut	40	30.00	1200.00	2014-07-20

If you execute the program in Listing 10.3, you will be prompted three times to enter the invoice's c_no, p_name, and invoice_dt you are querying. If the invoice is not available in the invoice table, the program will abort, and you will see a "no data found" error message, which looks like the following.

```
SQL0438N  Application raised error or warning with
      diagnostic text: "NO_DATA_FOUND".
```

To handle the error (exception), you can add an exception-handling statement to the program in Listing 10.3. Listing 10.4 shows a modified version of the program in Listing 10.3. There is an exception handler in the program in Listing 10.4.

Listing 10.4: With Exception Handling

```
DECLARE
   invc invoice%ROWTYPE;
BEGIN
   SELECT *
   INTO invc
   FROM invoice
   WHERE c_no                       = '&c_no_prompt'
   AND p_name                       = '&p_name_prompt'
   AND TO_CHAR(invoice_dt, 'DD-MON-YY') =
      '&invoice_dt_prompt';
   dbms_output.put_line(invc.c_name || ' - ' ||
      invc.p_name || ' - ' || invc.total_prc);
```

```
EXCEPTION
WHEN no_data_found THEN
  dbms_output.put_line('Error: The invoice does not
      exist!');
END;
```

If the invoice you are querying is not in the invoice table, the WHEN no_data_found will trap and handle the error, and displays its message. In other words, the program will not abort.

To see the exception-handler's message, issue a **set serveroutput on** command before you execute the program.

Stored Programs

You can store a PL/SQL program in the DB2 database. You can then call the stored program, such as in another PL/SQL program. Stored program comes in two types: function and procedure.

Stored Function

You learned Oracle built-in functions in Chapter 9, "Built-in Functions." Using PL/SQL you can write your own functions. The syntax for a stored function is as follows.

```
CREATE FUNCTION function name(parameters)
    RETURN data_type
  IS
    Variable_declarations
  BEGIN
    Processing_statements
  EXCEPTION
    Exception_handling statements
  END;
```

For example, Listing 10.5 shows the statement to create a stored function named f_calc_new_price. The function takes two parameters and uses the values of the parameters to calculate a new price and returns the result. If you execute the statement in Listing 10.5, a stored function named f_calc_new_price will be created and stored in your database.

Listing 10.5: Creating stored function calc_new_price

```
CREATE FUNCTION f_calc_new_price(
    exist_price NUMBER,
    change_percentage NUMBER)
  RETURN NUMBER
  IS
```

```
BEGIN
  RETURN exist_price + (exist_price *
    change_percentage);
END;
```

Now you can use the function just like you would any Oracle built-in function. The PL/SQL program in Listing 10.6 has an UPDATE statement that uses (calls) the calc_new_price function to calculate new prices and update the prices of all products.

Listing 10.6: Using the calc_new_price function

```
BEGIN
UPDATE product SET price = f_calc_new_price(price, 0.1) ;
END;
```

Stored Procedure

While a stored function returns a value, a stored procedure performs some actions. The syntax for creating a stored procedure is as follows.

```
CREATE PROCEDURE procedure_name(parameters)
  IS
    Variable_declarations
  BEGIN
    Processing_statements
  EXCEPTION
    Exception_handling statements
  END;
```

Listing 10.7 is an example statement for creating a stored procedure named p_calc_new_price. The procedure calculates a new price based on the values of its two parameters.

Listing 10.7: Creating stored procedure p_calc_new_price

```
CREATE PROCEDURE p_calc_new_price(
    p_code_par product.p_code%type,
    change_percentage NUMBER)
IS
  p_row product%ROWTYPE;
BEGIN
  SELECT * INTO p_row FROM product WHERE p_code = p_code_par;
  UPDATE product
  SET price    = p_row.price + (p_row.price *
      change_percentage)
  WHERE p_code = p_code_par;
END;
```

Now you can use (call) the procedure. Listing 10.8 is an example PL/SQL program. p_calc_new_price is called to update the price of the product with p_code = 1.

Listing 10.8: Calling the p_calc_new_price stored procedure

```
BEGIN
  p_calc_new_price(1, .05) ;
END;
```

Notice the difference on the use of function and procedure (Listing 10.6 versus Listing 10.8), the function returns a value that must be assigned to a variable (price); while, the procedure performs the price update directly.

Summary

In this chapter you learned several PL/SQL features. However, what's presented here is just the tip of the iceberg. PL/SQL has many other features that you will need in real-world application development. These other features are unfortunately beyond the scope of this book.

Chapter 11: Catalog

The catalog tables, commonly called data dictionary or metadata, has all data about our data in our database.

When you are writing queries, the catalog can be your reference for, for example, tables and their columns. You can query the DB2 catalog **view** to find out these data about them and others.

The catalog view is in the SYSCAT database, so to query, for example, what tables you have in your database, you run the following SELECT statement against the TABLES view:

Listing 11.1: Querying the Catalog View

```
SELECT * FROM SYSCAT.TABLES;
```

SYSCAT.TABLES

To find out the tables you own, query the SYSCAT.TABLES view. The query in Listing 11.2 returns the names of the tables owned by user DJONI.

Listing 11.2: Using the user_catalog view

```
SELECT tabname FROM SYSCAT.TABLES WHERE owner = 'DJONI'
    and type = 'T';
```

Type 'T' means the type of "table" we are querying is Table. The output from running the query in Listing 11.2 in your database may not be exactly the same as what I have got here. Here is mine.

```
TABNAME
----------
PRODUCT
CUSTOMER
SHIPMENT
C_ORDER
INVOICE
```

Note that this view, in addition to the *tabname* column, has many other columns.

SYCAT.COLUMNS

Querying the SYSCAT.COLUMNS gives you the data about columns. For example, the query in Listing 11.3 shows you the column names, and their data type, length, and scale, of the product table.

Listing 11.4: Finding out the columns metadata of the product table

```
SELECT colname, typename, length, scale FROM SYSCAT.COLUMNS
WHERE tabname='PRODUCT' order by COLNO;
```

Here is the query output.

```
COLNAME      TYPENAME       LENGTH    SCALE
----------   ----------   -----------  ------
P_CODE       VARCHAR            6         0
P_NAME       VARCHAR           15         0
PRICE        DECIMAL            4         2
LAUNCH_DT    DATE               4         0
```

In addition to these five columns, this view has many other columns, such as those for showing the null-ability and the default value.

SYSCAT.ROUTINES

The SYSCAT.ROUTINES view contains information about your stored functions and procedures. Use the query in Listing 11.5 to show your stored programs.

Listing 11.5: Revealing the metadata of stored procedures and functions

```
SELECT routinename, routinetype
FROM SYSCAT.ROUTINES
WHERE owner='DJONI';
```

Executing the query against your database will give you something like the following output rows, where routinetype F is Function.

```
ROUTINENAME          ROUTINETYPE
----------------   -----------
F_CALC_NEW_PRICE   F
P_CALC_NEW_PRUCE   F
```

The SYSCAT.ROUTINE has a TEXT column which contains the source code of the stored procedures and functions. For example, the query in Listing 11.6 returns the source code of the CALC_NEW_PRICE function.

Listing 11.6: Reading the source code of a function

```
SELECT text FROM SYSCAT.ROUTINE WHERE routinename =
    'F_CALC_NEW_PRICE';
```

Executing the query will show you the lines of codes of the function as shown here.

```
CREATE FUNCTION f_calc_new_price(
    exist_price DECIMAL(4,2), pct_change DECIMAL(1,0))
        RETURN DECIMAL
  IS
  BEGIN
    RETURN exist_price + exist_price * 0.1;
  END
```

Summary

The catalog contains the metadata of your database. In this chapter you learned to use some of the views in the data dictionary.

Appendix A: Installing IBM DB2 Express-C

To try out the examples in this book, you need a working DB2 database server and a client. Because you need to create tables and other objects, as well as store and update data, it is best if you have your own new installation. Fortunately, you can download DB2 Express-C Edition for free from IBM's website. As you will learn in this appendix, DB2 Express-C comes with a command-line client tool called CLPPlus that you can use to run SQL statements.

Downloading DB2 Express-C

DB2 Express-C software can be downloaded from this IBM web page.

```
http://www-01.ibm.com/software/data/db2/express-
    c/download.html
```

Select the version for your platform and follow the download instructions. You will be requested to sign in to your IBM account, and, if you don't have one already, create an account. Don't worry, creating an account is free.

Note

The book examples are tested on Windows. They should work equally well on UNIX and the other supported platforms. The following installation guide is for Windows only.

Installing DB2 Express-C

Run your downloaded file by double-clicking it; its file name will be similar to *v10.5fp1_win_expc.exe*. You might see the Open File –Security Warning like that in Figure A.1.

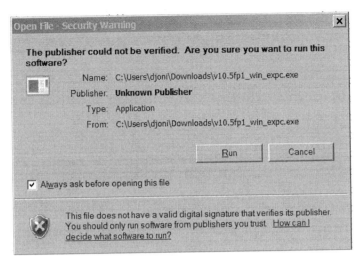

Figure A.1: The Open File - Security Warning

If you download the file from the IBM website, don't worry, click the Run button. The next window that will appear is your file extraction, which depends on the file extraction software you have; mine is the one in Figure A.2.

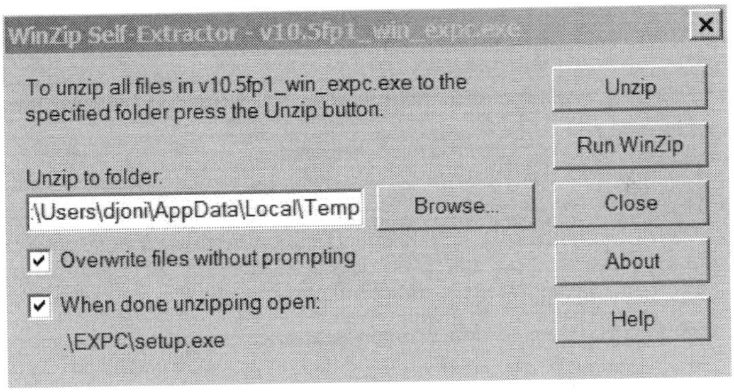

Figure A.2: File extraction

Click the Browse button and navigate to a directory of your choice. When you are done with the directory selection, and getting back to the file extraction window, click the Unzip button.

The next window after the completion of the file extraction is the Welcome screen as shown in Figure A.3.

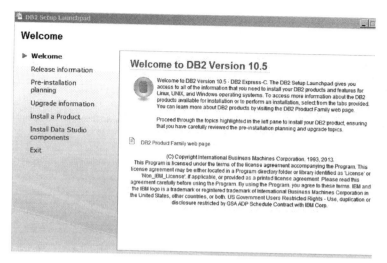

Figure A.3: Welcoming to DB2

Select "Install a Product" from the menu listed on the left side; your Welcome screen should now look like that shown in Figure A.4. Click the Install New button.

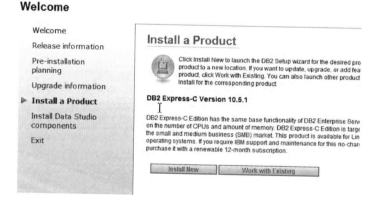

Figure A.4: The Summary window

When the Setup window appears (Figure A.5) click the Next button. Then, on the License Agreement window, accept the license agreement, and click the Next button.

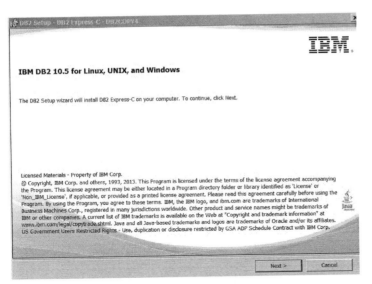

Figure A.5: Setup window

On the Installation Type window (Figure A.6), select Typical and click the Next button.

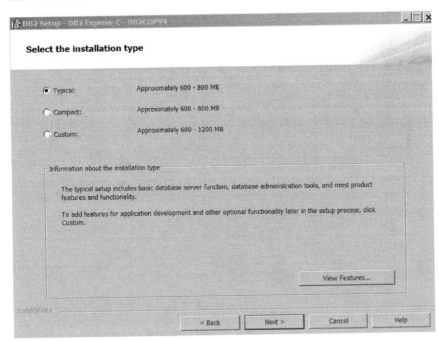

Figure A.6: Installation Type

On the next window (Figure A.7), select "Install DB2 Express-C on this computer" option, and click the Next button.

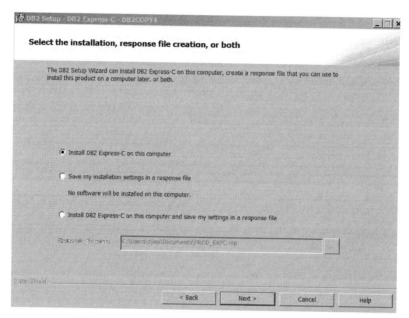

Figure A.7: Installation/Response File window

On the next window, select the location of your installation; and, then when the window similar to that shown in Figure A.8 appears, click the Next button. Click the Next button again on the DB2 Instances window.

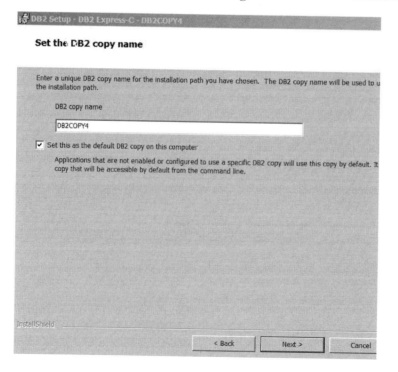

Figure A.8: DB2 copy name window

On the next window (Figure A.9), enter and confirm your password for the *db2admin* account; then, click the Next button.

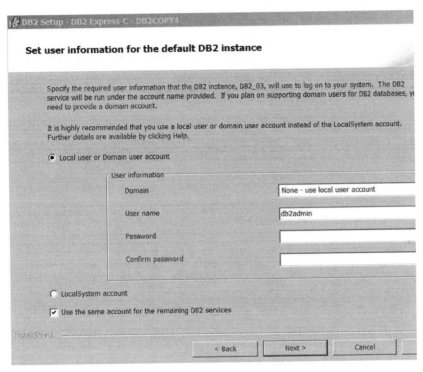

Figure A.9: db2admin password window

On the Start copying window (Figure A.10), click the Install button; and wait for the installation completion.

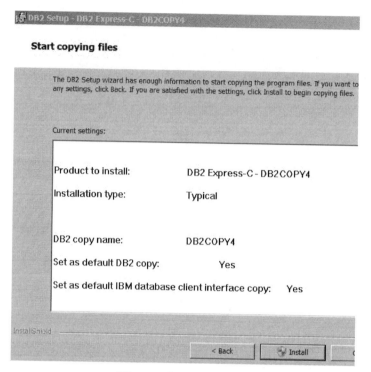

Figure A.10: Start copying window

When the Setup completion window appears (Figure A.11), click the Finish button, and your DB2 is ready for use.

You will next learn to use the CLPPlus command-line client.

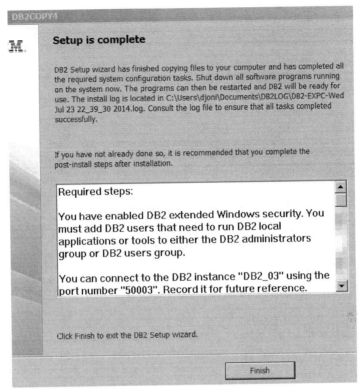

Figure A.11: Setup completion window

Using the CLPPlus

In this book you will use CLPPlus to interact with the DB2 database server.

Start the CLPPlus client command-line tool from the Windows start menu by selecting the DB2 Command Line Processor Plus.

Connect to the DB2 server using the account you use to log in to your Windows.

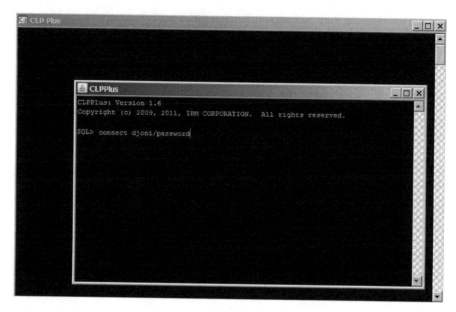

When prompted for DATABASE NAME, HOSTNAME and PORT, just press Enter key. At the SQL> prompt, you can type in SQL statements and run them.

Setting NULL Display

To see NULL data, rather than blank, issue a command: SET null NULL;

Before you issue the command, when you query a table, such as the product table, the output you see is as follows. Notice the blanks on the PRICE and LAUNCH_DT of the New Nut.

```
P_CODE P_NAME          PRICE LAUNCH_DT
------ --------------- ------ ----------
1      Nail            10.00 2013-03-31
2      Washer          15.00 2013-03-29
3      Nut             15.00 2013-03-29
4      Screw           25.00 2013-03-30
5      Super_Nut       30.00 2013-03-30
6      New Nut
```

After you issue the SET null NULL command, you will NULL instead of blank.

```
P_CODE P_NAME          PRICE LAUNCH_DT
------ --------------- ------ ----------
1      Nail            10.00 2013-03-31
2      Washer          15.00 2013-03-29
3      Nut             15.00 2013-03-29
4      Screw           25.00 2013-03-30
5      Super_Nut       30.00 2013-03-30
6      New Nut          NULL NULL
```

To close CLPPLus, enter and execute **EXIT** on the SQL prompt.

You are now set to test the book examples.

Made in the USA
Middletown, DE
08 June 2016